REVERENCE FOR LIFE AND FAMILY

PARENT/TEACHER BACKGROUND RESOURCE

Catechesis in Sexuality
John E. Forliti, D. Min.

Religious Education Division
Wm. C. Brown Company Publishers
Dubuque, Iowa

Nihil Obstat: Roy C. Lepak, STD
             Censor Deputatus

Imprimatur: +John R. Roach, DD
             Archbishop of St. Paul and Minneapolis

July 6, 1981

Illustration Credits

From Hole, J. W. Jr., *Human Anatomy and Physiology,* ©
1978, 1981, Wm. C. Brown Company Publishers, Dubuque,
Iowa—Figures A and B (left-bottom), Figure D (top).
Reprinted by permission.

From Mader, Sylvia S., *Inquiry into Life,* 2nd ed., © 1976,
1979, Wm. C. Brown Company Publishers, Dubuque,
Iowa—Figures C and D (bottom). Reprinted by permission.

Manufactured in the United States of America.
ISBN 697–01789–3

Contents

Foreword

From the moment of our birth our parents began to educate us in sexuality. The attitudes that we grew up with about male and female, self-worth, physical attributes and appearance, affection, emotion and passion, love, sexual powers and activities, and many other aspects of life—these attitudes were part of our earliest experience of life. Whether we were aware of it or not, our parents were giving us sex education.

Besides the attitudes, they taught us about sexuality by their statements of information and values. Even more so, perhaps, they taught us by the habits they tried to instill. Parents are the primary educators in sexuality.

This booklet is an attempt to assist parents, and their helpers in education—the teachers who have their children in class, in their role as moral educators. Today's culture and environment does not give as much support to moral educators as perhaps was the case a generation or two ago. This is unfortunate. It is our hope that the Life and Family program will encourage Christian parents and teachers, as well as Christian youth, to learn their heritage and to commit themselves to the strong and beautiful values and beliefs that are a part of it.

Moral education in sexuality is a very important need today, if the family is to survive. It is with a great deal of hope and excitement that we present this program of catechesis in sexuality. Realizing it could be improved in many ways, we hesitate to publish it. But, a start must be made sometime and with something. We offer this as a start then, a beginning effort, to get the wheels turning, the mind and heart moving. Life and family are two of the most precious gifts we are called to be stewards of—may the Lord assist us in this wonderful privilege.

Special thanks to the Life and Family Steering Committee, especially Father Mark Dosh who carefully reviewed this manuscript and made several helpful suggestions. Our gratitude also to members of the Catholic Education Center staff and to the facilitators and teachers of the pilot phase. Their contribution to the development of this booklet was essential.

Rev. John E. Forliti
June 24, 1979

1 Christian Marriage and Family

Meaghan's folks celebrated their silver anniversary last month. Some of their friends didn't think they would still be together for their twenty-fifth anniversary, but they have remained faithful, "through thick and thin," as the saying goes—committed to each other and their four children through plenty of trouble and arguments. Regular church-goers, their faith is simple, unsophisticated, and personal. They are looking forward to the wedding when they will escort Meaghan down the aisle.

Scott's parents have been divorced for seven years. When they pledged their vows, they seemed to have met all the requirements for the perfect marriage. Scott's dad still can't figure out what went wrong. His mother claims they started growing apart from the very beginning of their marriage. She remarried. Scott still sees his dad a lot—they were always close—and he has learned to accept his mother's new marriage. For their wedding, Meaghan and Scott have worked out, to everyone's satisfaction, who will accompany Scott's mother. Not every pair of newlyweds in this situation is so fortunate.

Knowing the pain of divorce in Scott's family, he and Meaghan are especially anxious to make their marriage work. They have taken advantage of all the opportunities offered by their church to prepare for the Sacrament of Matrimony. As they told a friend one day, "Marriage is a journey together through life. We want to be ready for the bumps and potholes as well as the ecstacy!"

Honesty is no less a good because some people fail to tell the truth. Fidelity is no less beautiful because it isn't always achieved. Justice is no less a virtue because you and I find it difficult to put into practice. The ideal remains whether or not we manage to live it.

With the prevalence of separation and divorce and the daily turmoils in which families find themselves, it becomes easier to deny the existence of the ideals of stable marriages and well-functioning families. Most adults today have good friends and acquaintances whose marriages and families seemed to have failed. Because of this, some hesitate to speak about the ideals of Christian marriage and family life with their children.

This failure to speak can add to the present dilemmas surrounding marriage. Young people need to have ideals presented to them, not in a sterile vacuum, unrelated to life, but in the context of reality. They also need to be helped to realize that no one lives any ideal perfectly. People are more or less honest, more or less loving, more or less virtuous. No one is perfect. But ideals are necessary to successful living. They lead us toward fulfillment; they draw us toward happiness and inner peace.

This chapter considers some of the ideals which our Christian tradition teaches about marriage and family. It considers the rich Christian tradition which has given and continues to give depth and substance to Christian family life. Elsewhere in this book, the single and celibate lifestyles will be considered, for these persons also have families to which they relate and belong. No matter what the reader's personal condition or life situation, marriage and family are precious creations of God which touch all our lives deeply. What does our Church teach about marriage and family?

1. God is the author of the marriage bond.
Who invented marriage? Whose idea was it first? The Bible teaches that it was God's idea, our Creator's invention. A bit of reflection about human nature might suggest the same an-

swer, called forth by the obvious beauty and power that there is in the image of a man and a woman, united in an inseparable bond, caring for each other and walking through life as companions. Human beings were not meant to be alone, Scripture says. The union of man and woman is similar to God's union with His chosen people. God freely bound Himself to them by a covenant. Out of love, He promised to be faithful to them; having given His word, He would keep it. They could rest, assured of His promise. Thus are two individuals meant to be in marriage; at rest, assured of the promise.

2. The root and foundation of a marriage is the consent which is freely given.

Marriage requires maturity—not perfection, rather maturity. Its serious responsibilities and demands necessitate the degree of autonomy and personal development required to make a prudent free choice. A man and a woman who realize sufficiently well what marriage is, freely choose to take each other as husband and wife. They are not forced, they do not just "fall into it," nor, must they be totally free of doubts. They are as free as is humanly possible; therefore, their decision can be said to be their own.

The partners take each other in faith, not knowing what the future holds. Faith is always a journey in darkness, not the darkness of night but the darkness of mystery. Faith provides light enough to choose a direction; moving toward the light, one knows not what lies ahead on the road, nor off to the sides, yet one chooses to move along anyway. Husband and wife freely join themselves in a conjugal convenant, for better or for worse, for richer or for poorer, in sickness and in health, until death.

They give their word. One reason why some marriages may have problems is that little value is attached to the giving and receiving of one's word. At a time when written contracts often are not taken very seriously, unwritten contracts may suffer even greater disavowal. To give my word to another is to contract with that other, to place my honor on the line, to invite the trust of the other. When the other person accepts my word, the contract is established. Marriage is contracted by a man and woman, each giving their word and accepting the other's word.

3. Marriage is an intimate partnership of life and love.

The Second Vatican Council, in Church in the Modern World, teaches that marriage is an intimate partnership of life and love. "Thus a man and a woman who by their compact of conjugal love 'are no longer two, but one flesh' render mutual help and service to each other through an intimate union of their persons and of their actions" (no. 48).

Recently the eldest son of a friend-couple was discussing life and love with his parents and his bride-to-be. At one point the son, age 23, summarized his belief as to what love was. Reflecting for a moment, then sharing her thoughts, the groom's mother looked at him tenderly and said, "Maybe so, but I think a couple has to be married fourteen years before they begin to understand what love really is."

Do couples give up too soon perhaps, just when their love is being tested and ready to grow by a leap? Maybe, maybe not; but the question deserves honest confrontation. Have you ever heard someone say, "I had no idea what I was getting into when I got married"? This statement might be applied to life in general. No one really knows what they're getting into— which is what makes the choice of any vocation an act of faith and trust.

4. Christian marriage requires fidelity, permanence, and openness to life.

Husband and wife freely bestow *self* on the other. This mutual self-giving imposes total fidelity in their relationship. Only God can take priority over their own relationship, which is exclusive and primary. No other human can take the place of one's spouse. The relationship is permanent, the promise made "until death do us part."

In an age when the possibility of permanent commitment is questioned, the Church insists on permanence, believing that such self-giving is both possible and laudable. When two individuals give themselves to each other in marriage and accept each other, by that mutual expression, they give rise to a relationship which "by divine will and in the eyes of society is a lasting one" (The Church in the Modern World, no. 48). Besides requiring fidelity and permanence of the couple, the Church insists on openness to life. Marriage does not exist solely for the welfare of the couple, but is a social sacrament and therefore looks beyond itself. Marriage looks outward to the creation of new life and to the nurturing of life. We must not forget, therefore, that Christian marriage, being a social sacrament, is intended for the building up of the Body of Christ.

5. The coessential purposes of marriage are union and procreation.
Prior to the Second Vatican Council, the theology of marriage stressed the creation of new life as the primary purpose of marriage. Afterwards it emphasized two purposes of marriage, both of them essential and equally important, namely, the union of the spouses and procreation of new life. This conciliar teaching is of utmost importance and possibly represents one of the most significant developments of Catholic thought in recent times. (Chapter eleven develops this teaching.)

6. Children are the "ultimate crown" of marriage and conjugal love.
In the book of Genesis, God commands Adam and Eve "to increase and multiply." They did; so did those who followed. The Council teaches that children are the supreme gift of marriage (Church in the Modern World, no. 50) and places a high value on new human life. Children are not seen as a burden, no matter what difficulties they present, but rather as a gift contributing to the welfare of the parents. Our faith teaches that a child is the visible fruit of conjugal love. This is not to

5

say that childless marriages are second-class. Rather, because of the tremendous dignity of human life and the immortal value of the human being, the procreation and nurturing of a child is appreciated as a supreme good—but not the only good.

Some couples are not able to bear children. Others, for a variety of reasons, realize that their circumstances make it unwise or even irresponsible to have children. Such circumstances may be temporary or permanent, but the marriage is no less a marriage because of it. For reasonable and serious cause, childless couples are called to live out the procreative purpose of marriage in a more indirect fashion, for example, by fostering as best they can those less fortunate than themselves. In some Christian marriages, openness to life will be realized in ways other than the blessing of children.

7. Marriage and the family are the foundation of society.

The Second Vatican Council called marriage and the family the most basic and fundamental units of society (Church in the Modern World, no. 52). It is easy to see why the Council spoke of the family as a "community of love." Husband and wife, bound to each other in marriage, establish a basic community of love in which they live with and for each other. When a child is born or adopted into this community of love, the child is blessed with optimum conditions for healthy growth and development. Mother and father form the human cradle of love, providing for the child the security and care it needs to get a good start in life. How well we realize today the importance of the first years in the shaping of the adult human being.

8. The family is a community of love, the first and most important school of life.

Christian spouses, sustained by God's loving presence and by their participation in the mystery of Christ's love for His Church, "help each other to attain to holiness in their married life and in the rearing and education of their children" (Constitution on the Church, no. 11). If the family is to accomplish its mission, the mother and father must collaborate very closely in bringing up their children. The Council stated in the document, The Church in the Modern World, that "the active presence of the father is highly beneficial to their formation" and that the "children, especially the younger among them, need the care of their mothers at home" (no. 52). Both of these statements provide much food for thought and discussion.

A recent study revealed the shocking fact that many infants receive almost no intimate time with their young executive fathers, so totally immersed were the fathers in their careers, and almost totally uninvolved in the care and feeding of their babies. The other side of the coin is mothers of young children working outside the home. In some situations adults other than the parents are called upon to provide an intimate presence to the infant and young child, at least for a time.

The child has a natural right to have a father and a mother, a recent Vatican publication, the 1978 report of the Papal Committee for the Family, stated. This concept is the best starting point in a discussion on single parenting. It is closest to the ideal and the way things should be if they can. Obviously, they can't always be ideal. I have watched a single mother of three children, widowed when the oldest child was five and the youngest child three months, bring up her offspring to adulthood. Each child has turned out as well as any child reared by both parents, and raising the children was a supremely challenging task at times. Yet, she did it. Even so, her children missed having a father and may wonder for the rest of their lives how it might have been had he lived.

Literature abounds with examples showing the unique and essential role both parents have in raising wholesome and well-functioning humans. As we consider the ideal family and environment for children, however, we must avoid setting too lofty a set of expectations. One does not have to go far to find young adults today who express serious reservations about their capacity to be good mothers and fathers, believing apparently that they don't have whatever parenthood requires. They may be overexpecting of themselves. Parents are not born, they are made; and probably parents' greatest teachers are their children. Parenting is a skill that develops over time and with experience. Though some would like to learn parenting first and then have the experience, God has not designed it so. Parents are forever destined to be shaped by their children!

9. The Church is also a community of love and a school of life. The Church is a community of love. Born in Baptism, the Christian is nourished in many ways, but especially at the table of the Lord in the Sacrament of the Eucharist. Jesus chose a simple meal and the sharing of simple foods, bread and wine, as the sign of His abiding love and presence for all time. The Eucharistic altar table is the center around which the family of faith and hope and love gathers regularly. At Eucharist Jesus binds His family together, filling His followers with His Spirit, a Spirit that enables them to say "Our Father, who art in heaven, hallowed be Thy Name."

A few years ago, while visiting with MaMa D (Giovanna D'Agostino), a renowned Italian cook, I expressed my concern over the breakdown of family life. I asked her "What's happening to families?" She replied, "You want to know what's destroying family life? TV dinners. There's no love in the food! It's the one who puts love in the food that glues the family together." I understood, not only something true of my own parents and their tremendous capacity to put love in the food, but of my God and the meaning of Eucharist.

One reason why some Christians have difficulty appreciating Eucharist is that they lack sufficient experience with family meals. Jesus was clear in revealing that love is our highest calling. "Which is the greatest commandment? . . . love the Lord your God with all your heart, all your mind, and all your will . . . and love your neighbor as yourself" (Matthew 22:36). The Church and family are two communities of love that can influence lives in beautiful and significant ways. Youth share in the privileges as well as the responsibilities that this gift entails. Jesus calls the Church to transcend even the bounds of family.

Because you are God's chosen ones, holy and beloved, clothe yourselves with heartfelt mercy, with kindness, humility, meekness, and patience. Bear with one another; forgive whatever grievances you have against one another. Forgive as the Lord has forgiven you. Over all these virtues put on love, which binds the rest together and makes them perfect. Christ's peace must reign in your hearts, since as members of the one body you have been called to that peace. Dedicate yourselves to thankfulness (Colossians 3:12–16).

No one's family is perfect; neither is anyone's marriage. They cannot be perfect. Life is made up of weeds and wheat. Living rooms get messy, especially if they are lived in. Marriages and families are sometimes ragged and frequently less than harmonious. Still, our family is our family. It's what we have and it's what we are, to a great extent. Whether or not a family is broken, blended, together, torn, extended, nuclear, single-parent, alcoholic, poor, middle-class, monied, intimate, unaffectionate, or whatever, if it is my family, it is special and it is precious. Ideals should not be used to judge and condemn, but rather to help us keep our eyes on the positive and the good. Ideals are God's way of saying, "Keep looking upward and ahead. You are called to be the best you can be."

LESSON 1   LIST OF TERMS

Community

Unified body of individuals, organized to some degree for a common purpose or interchange.

Conjugal Love

Love of husband and wife, binding them together in the union of marriage. *Conjugal* is a word which means "joined, yoked, bound together."

Covenant

Formal, solemn, and binding agreement. In Judaeo-Christian tradition *covenant* refers to the relationship between God and His people, a relationship of love initiated by God and calling for a faith response from the people. God's love is freely given, faithful, and permanent.

Family

The basic unit of society ordinarily understood to mean parents and their children. An extended family includes relatives such as grandparents, uncles, aunts, cousins, etc. (Families with one-parent in the home are referred to as single-parent families; families formed when one parent with children marries another parent with children are referred to as blended families.)

Fidelity

Quality or state of being faithful. Fidelity in marriage means that the relationship between husband and wife is special and exclusive. Husband and wife express their fidelity in many ways, one of which is sexual intimacy.

Christian Marriage

A man and a woman (usually both baptized Christians) join in a special social, legal, and spiritual relationship through their mutual and irrevocable personal consent. It is a sacrament of the Catholic Church whereby Christ is present to the couple as they live out the unitive and procreative purposes of marriage.

Openness to Life	Husband and wife recognize their call to be generous towards others, and they will accept children lovingly as gifts from God, giving them a loving home in which to grow.
Permanence	Marriage vow is intended to be kept until death.
Relationship	Specific type of kinship; a connection between two or more people.
Reverence	Ability to treat someone or something as each should be treated, according to its own beauty and truth.

2 Birth into Family and Church

The weather that day was hot and humid. At work, Steve had worried about Melanie. Overdue a week, she appeared tired and very uncomfortable that morning. Expecting their first baby, they noted nearly every kick and stir. That evening Melanie looked radiant, as expectant mothers so often do. Would it be tonight for them?

Events have a way of turning suddenly. Melanie retired early while Steve, still in a pensive mood, settled in his favorite chair and paged through the daily newspaper, his mind actually on the baby and his wife. Breaking the stillness, Melanie called to him. Her time had come! He knew exactly what he had to do, having rehearsed it a thousand times in his imagination.

Assured by the nurses, expectant father and mother performed perfectly. The safe delivery of a healthy child filled their hearts with an indescribable joy. Steve momentarily recalled yesterday's anxiety when, for a long painful moment, he had lingered over a thought he wanted no part of. What if the baby were not all right? He laughed now as he dismissed yesterday's worries.

"This is our baby, our baby," the young parents repeated in their hearts. "We'll do our best! We'll be good parents. Thanks, God! You are so good!"

For some today, delivering a baby is a family affair. Attentive to the child during pregnancy, the father and occasionally even older children are present and active during the hours of labor and delivery. It's not exactly a return to giving birth at home, but almost! Many prospective parents object to Mom having her child at the hospital without her husband present. Consequently, about three out of ten fathers prepare for and assist in the delivery of their babies. Also, contemporary medical practice often has the mother fully alert and active in the birthing process.

Strange as it may sound, the same trend toward greater family involvement is true of infant Baptism. Not very long ago it was common for godparents to take the infant to church to be baptized. Mom stayed home to continue recuperation; or if she went to church, she and Dad took a secondary role. Contemporary practice puts both parents right up front, holding their infant and expressing their own intention to raise the child in the Faith.

Another change that characterizes couples of child-bearing age today is the amount of thought and deliberation that surrounds their decision to have a child. For the most part, since human history began, couples simply "took what came." Today, when much is known about the process of reproduction and birth, couples have many more factors to consider than generations before them apparently had to think about.

In addition to the changing attitudes and customs described previously, the value of human life itself may have been severely weakened in our society as a direct result of the 1973 Supreme Court decision concerning abortion. Indeed, some suggest that a strong antichild mentality exists in the United States today.

What do Catholics believe about the value of a child? What can be learned from the process of fetal development and the experiences of birth? What does the Church teach about the developing and the newborn child? This chapter presents several Christian principles and beliefs surrounding the conception and birth of a child.

1. Life is a gift.

The breath of life has been given by the Creator to all living creatures. Living things did not earn life, nor did any creature do anything to deserve it. Life is simply and totally a gift. Living creatures depend upon God for life. To believe that life is a gift is to believe that we cannot do with it whatever we want. The intention and purpose of the Giver must be respected. No human has complete and total rights over any life, including his or her own.

2. Life is a responsibility.

Not only is life a gift, it is also a responsibility. Each person is responsible to God for his or her life. Furthermore, a person can be responsible to God for the life of another whenever that other person cannot care for him- or herself. This responsibility is most obvious in the case of a small child, an elderly person, or a handicapped individual.

Recently I conducted a course in morality for adults and gave some reading material to the participants in preparation for the next class. The class opened with a young father objecting to the use of *should* and *ought* in the material. He insisted that these words were archaic and should not be used. I insisted they had to be used.

I asked, "If your two-year-old child was walking towards the street, heading for obvious danger, and a neighbor just stood by without rushing to protect the child, wouldn't you feel that he or she should have made an attempt to preserve the child's safety?" The answer was obvious—responsible persons would feel that they ought to see to the child's welfare. Morality deals with "shoulds" and "oughts."

A child has a claim on others for the nurturing and preservation of its life. The same is true for the elderly who are no longer able to care for themselves, and for the handicapped and others who lack the ability to care for themselves. Such persons have a claim on the rest of us. No one, neither singly or collectively, may deny another person's basic right to life.

3. A child is born first a member of natural creation.
The sacred Scriptures teach that from the beginning mankind was made in the image of God, created and blessed with goodness. "And God saw that it was good" (Genesis 1:31). Human beings easily see themselves as a part of a larger creation. The physical universe with its galaxies and planets, the planet earth with its mountains and oceans are marvelous works of God, awesome to behold, magnificent in their beauty, but we can also easily see the marvelous creation which is ourselves. Christian tradition understands man and woman to be the crowning glory of the Divine creation, imaging the Creator especially in the power to think and to love.

4. The condition of separation and disorder in "fallen nature" call for God's gift of redemption.
Sacred Scripture also teaches that something went awry in the original harmony that existed in mankind. St. Paul expressed it well when he described the battle going on within himself. "What happens is that I do, not the good that I will to do, but the evil I do not intend" (Romans 7:19). This conflict arose through the first man's fault, and everyone since that time experiences that interior struggle. In this respect, everyone resembles Adam. In I Corinthians (15:45 ff) St. Paul tells us that Adam, the first human person, was of earth, formed from dust; the second Adam (that is, Christ) is from heaven. Earthly people are like the person of earth, heavenly people are like the one from heaven. Just as we resemble the one from earth (Adam), so shall we bear the likeness of the one from heaven (Christ). Original sin is the term given to the condition of separation from God, the lack of sanctifying grace, and the tendency to disorder within men and women.

5. Baptism and grace bestow a new birth on a child.

To redeem us from our separation and alienation from our Creator, God sent His son, Jesus. Jesus, the new Adam, is the firstborn of the new creation, a creation of faith and grace. This new creation is not cosmetic, superficial, or "tacked on." It is a change in being, a true transformation from one state of being to another. Baptized into the Body of Christ, we are taken out of the realm of sin and immersed into the very "bloodstream" of God, God's life. This is why we speak of ourselves as children of God, as members of Jesus' own body on this earth. As children of God, we can truly say that Jesus is our brother and God is our Father. With Jesus now, we can call God, "Our Father." We can say "Abba, Father," a term that expresses an intimate and personal relationship with God. We can say that we have been "reborn" into the divine life, by Baptism, taken into the family of God, the divine community of love. When we are divinely adopted, we are given the powers of knowing (faith), awaiting (hope), and loving (charity), as God would have His child know, await, and love.

In a real way, the Christian is empowered to see "with the eyes of God" and to love "with the heart of God." God shares His very own power with His children, enabling them to live a new life on this earth and one that continues into eternity. We are already able to breathe the air of the heavenly Kingdom, transformed by Baptism and faith into the People of God.

6. Born of nature and grace, the Christian child is nurtured by family and Church.

The Christian child is born into two communities of love, namely, the family and the Church. The Rite of Baptism for children, welcoming the child into God's family, highlights the role that the parents will play in bringing the child to the knowledge and love of God. The family is recognized as the child's first community of faith, with the parents celebrated as the "first teachers of their child in the ways of faith" (Blessing,

16

Rite of Baptism). An important concept to understand is that the creative work of parents extends for fifteen to twenty years, as they gradually lead the child into human maturity and Christian faith. A newborn baby requires the constant care and guidance of its parents if it is to grow as a human person, developing personal qualities of head and heart, and the capacities necessary for a fully human life in society. Parents try to guide their children to live purposefully as human beings, in ways that are meaningful and fulfilling.

Baptism makes similar demands of parents. The newly-baptized infant requires the guidance and sharing of its parents. As they live the life of faith and share this faith with their children, parents continue the work begun in Baptism. Baptism is a new birth, a birth of water and the Holy Spirit. By it, the child receives the redemptive grace of Jesus Christ and the right to grow into a full flowering of that grace. The parents are assured of God's help and loving presence, as they are encouraged to trust in God and live in the consciousness of His providential love.

The local Church community in which the child's Baptism takes place becomes "family" for the child. The child has a right to the love and help of the community, especially to a share in the community's faith. Godparents represent the Church to the child and remain as constant reminders of the child's new "family," the Church community.

7. Once conception occurs, the development of new human life proceeds in a marvelous and awesome manner.
New life begins with one miniscule cell which, by two months, will have multiplied 40,000 times, and by nine months will consist of 200 billion cells! After fertilization in the fallopian tube the embryo moves down and implants in the mother's uterus. Soon a protective covering surrounds it and a liquid cushion protects the tiny being from jolts and shocks. Nourished by its mother it grows at a phenomenal rate. At four

weeks it is only one-fourth of an inch long, but its spinal column is evident. At eight weeks, and about an inch long, its heart is pumping blood through its own body, and the eyes, ears, nose, and mouth have taken form. The limbs, having begun to appear at five weeks, are developed and moving at sixteen weeks.

Now called a fetus, and weighing about one-third of a pound, this new human life continues its marvelous development until about the end of the fifth month when its development is complete. Now it only needs to get larger and stronger. At nine months it is ready to be born. In a relatively brief time since conception, an incredible pace and pattern of development has occurred. It is awesome to behold.

8. Giving birth and rearing a child is a sacred event and privilege which is the right and responsibility of the father as well as the mother.

Contemporary child-rearing practices emphasize the importance of the father's role. This mutual parenting is encouraged in order to form strong bonds not only between the child and mother but also between child and father. Many couples today find it challenging to work out their mutual roles in the feeding, holding, teaching, disciplining, and general up-bringing of children. With mothers working outside the home now in greater numbers, couples find themselves searching out the merits and demerits of nursery schools, child-care facilities, and other parent-surrogates. Differences of opinion exist on the relative advantages and disadvantages of bringing adults other than the parents into child-care. Not only is the father's role up for discussion today, but so is the mother's and the surrogate's. Many questions raised in these discussions are new for our society, and it will probably take time before adequate data are collected to substantiate or challenge the various views and opinions.

9. How much should children be told about sex?

A question frequently asked, its answer depends very much on the individuals involved. Two guidelines are offered by way of illustrations. For example, a person who stands too close to a rose or a work of art may miss its full impact or receive a distorted view of the object under study. The same may happen with a friendship: Getting too close by way of overanalysis can have negative results, even possibly destroying the friendship. Perhaps God has built a "law of distance" into life. If this is true, and I suggest it is, this will be one of the factors parents and teachers must deal with as they guide the young in their curiosity and need for information about sexual matters. It would seem to be impossible to set down absolute rules defining the exact amount of information appropriate to every group or all individuals. Good sense and prudence must always be exercised, remembering that the "law of distance" has two extremes to be avoided: Too close or too far.

A second illustration comes from a statement made by a wise Catholic layman, Frank Sheed. He insists that sex always retains the quality of dynamite, like a powder keg that is by nature potentially explosive, which, if a spark touches it, may be unexpectedly set off. This image suggests that whenever the subject of sex is discussed or explored, the possibility of passion being aroused is present. Arousal itself may not be wrong, but it may be the start of something that could develop into more than was anticipated or intended.

Yes, there may be dangers involved in discussing and teaching the young about sex, just as there may be dangers in not teaching them about sex. Keeping in mind the two illustrations above, a few more specific guidelines can be offered:

a. Answer the child's questions, directly, simply, and with the details that are necessary.

b. Be sure you understand the question being asked and what it is the child really wants to know.

c. It is more important to emphasize values than anatomy. Teaching the principles underlying a wholesome Christian understanding of sex is best begun even before passion begins to stir.

Is it better to teach too much, too soon, rather than too little, too late? Neither situation is preferred, obviously. Adults responsible for children and youth simply have to work at providing the proper information at the appropriate times. Mistakes may be made, but the greatest mistake is to do nothing at all.

LESSON 2   LIST OF TERMS

Birth Canal
Passageway from the uterus to the vaginal opening, through which the baby moves in the process of birth.

Conception
Term given to the union of sperm and ovum (egg) which results in the beginning of new life.

Embryo
Organism in the earliest stages of its development, beginning with conception.

Fertilization
Union of a male sperm and female egg to begin a new life. (Another term for *conception*.)

Fetus
Term used for human life developing in the womb from the latter part of the third month until birth.

Legal Age
In some states, eighteen years old. Normally parents have responsibility for the child until he or she reaches legal age (i.e., age of majority).

Mutual Parenting
Shared in common; mother and father share parenting responsibilities and roles.

Ovum
Female egg, produced in the ovary. If a sperm cell fertilizes an ovum, the woman becomes pregnant.

Pregnancy
State of carrying a developing baby in the uterus. Normal length of a pregnancy is nine months.

Procreation
God invites human persons to join Him in the creation of new life. Procreation is more than reproduction since it involves the loving choice of the parents and the creative power of God in bringing forth a new, unique human being.

Reproduction
Process of continuing the species.

Semen
Fluid containing sperm ejaculated at male orgasm. Millions of spermatazoa are released in a single ejaculation.

Sperm
Male reproductive cells produced in the testes. Only one sperm is needed to fertilize an ovum.

Vagina
Female birth canal and organ for sexual intercourse.

3 From Child to Adult

Susan felt for a long time that she was a "slow developer." That's what Jim once called her. Not in an unkind way, but more as though he really knew how embarrassed she got at times and he was trying to soften the hurt.

Fourteen years old and she had not experienced "it" yet ("it" being her menstrual period). The doctor said she was normal and assured her that the signs of change were beginning to appear. What a relief! For her mother as well, who had done all she could to support Susan ever since that day three years earlier when Susan's friends made such a big deal out of their "arrival." Susan was more angry than depressed. Mom understood.

Jim wasn't so lucky. His dad died the summer he finished seventh grade. He was sure his mother knew he was filling out and becoming a man; but they couldn't talk about it. For a long time he thought there was something wrong with him. Too embarrassed to ask anyone, he learned from anyone he could. He finally drew some conclusions and decided that he must be normal! Still he had a lot of questions.

Biology class helped, of course, as did the conversations with the older boys last summer at the park. Some of them had their own vans, with really plush interiors! Wow! It must feel great to have your own wheels and all the girls saying you're really neat!

How did grandma's and grandpa's generations make it through adolescence when it wasn't treated as a big deal? Today, youth are studied, surveyed, analyzed, graphed, interviewed and filmed, all in an effort to understand them. Is it only our own times that have been baffled by its young ones? In the "good old days" did children grow up into adults without passing through the rugged detour of adolescence?

No doubt about it, life is more complicated today. Older generations passed from childhood to adulthood, then into old age.

Three stages at most, it seemed! As presently described, the human starts off in the oral stage, moves on through the anal stage to the genital and phallic stages, the identity stage, followed by the intimacy stage, and finally into the generativity and integrative stages. This is Harvard psychologist Erik Erikson's eight-stage schema of human development. It could easily appear that things are indeed more complex.

Contemporary society highlights adolescence and, in fact, has built a "sub-culture" around it. Consequently, parents, teachers, and others whose lives are interwoven with teenagers feel the separation caused by this subculture and are frequently at a loss as to how to deal with it. Is it more difficult today than a few generations ago to be a teenager? or the parents of a teenager? Perhaps, perhaps not. One thing seems certain, however: most teens (and their parents) survive the experience and move on to productive and fulfilling adulthood.

1. The onset of puberty triggers a series of changes which transform the child into an adolescent and gradually into an adult.
The fact that a human being is male or female is determined by a group of cells called gonads. The gonads develop into testes in a boy child and into ovaries in a girl child. The hypothalamus releases a hormone in both boys and girls and flows through special blood vessels to the pituitary gland. The pituitary gland, in turn, produces another hormone, which passes

through the bloodstream to the testes in the male where it stimulates male sex hormones and sperm. A second message from the pituitary gland directs the testes to produce the male sex hormone which is called testosterone. The second message from the pituitary gland in the young girl releases the female hormone called estrogen. When testosterone and estrogen are released into the bloodstreams of the young man and young woman, many physical and psychological changes take place. This time in life is called the age of puberty. It occurs in most girls between the age of ten to twelve and in boys between twelve to fourteen years.

The first pituitary secretion, a *f*ollicle *s*timulating *h*ormone, is the same in both male and female. FSH, as it is often abbreviated, initiates sperm production in the male and maturation of the ova (eggs) in the female. We say "maturation of the ova" in the female because while the male child is born with the organs which will produce sperm, the female child is born with all of the ova which will be expelled or fertilized during her lifetime. The immature ova are protected by a delicate covering of cells called follicular cells. In the male, the second hormone initiated by the pituitary gland and producing testosterone energizes a special group of cells in the testes called an *I*nterstitial *C*ell-*S*timulating *H*ormone. It is often abbreviated ICSH.

2. In addition to production of sex hormones and sperm and to maturation of the ova, numerous changes occur in males and females which are more obvious and external.
These are called secondary sex characteristics. In the female they are: increase in the rate of growth, widening of the pelvis, enlargement of breasts, increased fat giving rounded contours to the body, growth of pubic and underarm hair, discharge of mucus from the vaginal opening, and menstruation. In the male they are: deepening of the voice, relatively rapid increase in height and weight, longer bones, overgrowth of tougher skin,

broadening of the shoulders and general muscular development, growth of facial and pubic hair, increase in size of penis and testes, erection and ejaculation, nocturnal emissions, and increased metabolism.

Body structure and function depend principally upon heredity; that is, they are the result of the entire sociological strain that caused the quality of the sperm and ovum of a person's parents. Color of hair, eyes, texture of skin, length and weight of bones are some of the factors determined by the union of the sperm and ovum of a person's parents, their parents, and the parents before them. There are, however, other factors which cause differences in body growth rate and size. Some races tend to have large bony structures, while others have slight and small bones. Also, poorly nourished persons of any race will not develop as rapidly as well-nourished persons. Female maturity occurs earlier in climates that are warm and later in cold climates.

3. Adolescents have the physical capacity to conceive and bear children.

Emotional, moral, intellectual, social, and spiritual capacities must also develop and mature, however, before adolescents are ready to be responsible parents. Youth should be cautioned by parents and other caring adults that physical sexual development is only one aspect. Growth in all other dimensions is crucial for fulfilling relationships and responsible mature living.

Both boys and girls will appreciate adults who assure them early in puberty that nocturnal emissions and menstruation are perfectly normal. Calm assurances that stained bed sheets and underclothing are part of the normal course of life are very helpful. Boys should realize that it is the temporary intensity of their developing genital urge that causes involuntary erections, often unrelated to any direct sexual stimulus. The frequency of these involuntary occurrences will diminish in young manhood. Girls will appreciate basic information and guidance in the use of sanitary napkins, tampons, and feminine hygiene.

4. During adolescence both girls and boys experience many new feelings linked to physical changes.

Most adolescents feel awkward and self-conscious, some more than others. Intensely interested in physical appearance, they worry over acne, skin blemishes, hair, and clothing styles. They often feel insecure and lonely, sometimes experiencing extreme changes of mood. Peer approval and a sense of belonging are very important to them.

Girls may tend to desire physical closeness more while boys may feel an urgency to use their genital sexual capacity. Girls and boys seem to want attention; both cherish the freedom to be adventurous. They teeter between dependence and independence, fearing failure while anxious to succeed. Boys experience embarrassment when their voices change and deepen. Delighted at the prospect of becoming totally responsible for their lives, adolescents sometimes feel overwhelmed at the weight of it all. Yet, they manage, as their parents did before them.

5. Adolescent development is always unique to the individual.

Not all of the above characteristics are common to each individual adolescent, nor is one of them common to all young persons. Generally speaking, however, there is at this time of development a desire on the part of most young people to "try their wings." They want to experiment and to do things on their own. This can be frightening for parents and teachers because they realize that the lack of experience and skills make the young risk-taker vulnerable to failure and pain.

Yet, experience is essential to learning, and if young persons are given limited and guided opportunities to gradually discover their strengths and weaknesses, the possibility of serious failure and hurt can be reduced. The young person eager to experiment must understand that responsibility always accompanies the opportunity to try new behaviors. Learning that responsibility and behavior go hand in hand is one of the tasks of adolescence.

6. Development is necessary in each of six dimensions for the adolescent.

The following diagram may help explain what adolescents experience. We humans are complex creatures. There are several dimensions that make up who and what we are. These dimensions are difficult to distinguish at all times, and we use more than one way to define and describe ourselves. Some will prefer fewer categories than are given in the accompanying grid:

Dimensions	Adolescent growth and development from childhood to maturity
Physical	————————————————→
Intellectual	——————————————→
Emotional	——————→
Spiritual (religious faith)	———————→
Moral	——————————→
Social	———————————————→

The typical teen's development profile will be uneven. This is normal. What is worth noting about the unevenness of growth in the various dimensions is that it is important to grow in all areas if one is to reach full maturity. Some teens develop physically quite early while their emotional growth may lag far behind. Others develop faster intellectually than they do physically or emotionally. Some are slower developing their moral life, or their spiritual life, or social life. And so on.

7. Holistic growth is an important goal for young people.

The grid provided can help parents to understand their adolescent's behavior and perhaps to help the child grow in a more balanced manner. It can also help the adolescent. For example, in the area of sexual activity, a young person may appear ready physically and socially but may not be ready morally. Or another person may be physically and emotionally mature but not socially and morally. Throughout adolescence, emphasis should be placed on total growth, holistic development, a growth and development that is balanced and fully human.

8. Adolescents need special assurance, affirmation, and support.

Adolescents often worry or are embarrassed if they are not as tall or as developed as peers of the same chronological age. Discussion of the causes of different rates of growth and the assurance that these differences are normal will allay some of the "sexual fears" that are common during adolescence. It might be well to mention here that although an ovum (egg) may not be released by the ovaries the first few times a girl menstruates, it is important to know that a girl is capable of releasing an ovum. This means that when she reaches the age when she begins to menstruate, she is able to become pregnant if sperm from the male enters her body.

9. Unfortunately, some of the feedback at this time of physical and psychological growth is negative—from both parents and teachers.

The more negative responses and the more failures experienced, the more difficult it is to form a positive concept of self. It is not unusual, then, that an adolescent who does not find affirmation at home or at school, will seek and value it from peers. The young person will see himself or herself as lovable or unlovable as he or she is loved by others. Adolescents need to hear at this age that parents and teachers are *for* them, that is, on their side, not against them. An attitude that expresses itself in terms of warfare is most unfortunate and harmful to growth, though it is understandable how a teenager at times might feel attacked, given the tugging and pulling that normal development seems to require.

LIST OF TERMS

Ejaculation	Male discharge of semen.
Erection	Term used to describe the penis when it is filled with blood, and firm.
Genitalia	External sexual organs.
Hormone	Chemical produced by glands in the body, such as the pituitary, the testes, the ovaries.
Implantation	Cells of the fertilized ovum attach themselves to the cavity formed in the endometrium.
Labor	Name given to the final contractions of the uterus which stretch the cervix and force the baby through the birth canal.
Menopause	Final cessation of the menses; change of life; usually occurs between forty-five and fifty years of age.
Menstruation	The discharge of the soft, blood-filled tissue in the uterus which occurs about every twenty-eight days (sometimes less or more days), if the ovum is not fertilized.
Miscarriage	Name given to the discharge of the fetus for reasons beyond external control.
Ovulation	Release of a mature ovum from the ovary.
Pituitary Gland	Small, oval, two-lobed vascular body attached to the front center of the brain.
Placenta	Vascular structure by which the fetus is nourished in the uterus, and discharged from the woman's body after giving birth.
Puberty	Name given to the time of adolescence when hormonal changes take place resulting in secondary sex characteristics.
Sexual Intercourse	In a loving embrace the husband's penis is placed in the vagina of his wife. By this act they express their love, and if pregnancy occurs, they continue the human race.

Umbilical Cord	Cordlike, anatomical connection between the unborn baby and the placenta.
Wet Dreams	Involuntary ejaculations in a male occuring during sleep (nocturnal emissions), sometimes accompanied by dreams and/or sexual fantasy. The male body releases excess semen this way.

4 Wholeness and Sexual Integration

Coral and Gene were delighted the day their sixteen-year-old, David, threw away his cigarettes and lighter and announced his decision to "never indulge again." Having tried to quit at age 27 and again at age 39, Gene hoped the boy would stop smoking now before he really got hooked.

They both knew what it meant to indulge, and they also realized what it meant to quit. Coral went through treatment for chemical dependency just a year ago. Her alcoholism nearly cost her an office management position, her otherwise happy marriage, and her integrity. Thank God, they listened to George Nelson, a converted alcoholic himself. Their lives were much smoother now.

David's smoking had worried them, as did his conversations with his buddies. If Coral and Gene didn't know the parents of David's friends, they might have worried even more. It must be just "teen talk," they decided, "keggers," getting "zonked," and similar references. Coral and Gene had memories of their own harmless escapades, though they were a few years older than David and his friends when they had held their "beer busts" at the Pavilion.

Besides, hasn't David seen enough drinking in his own house to know better? Surely, he's not into drugs, or sex, or. . . . Some nagging questions hovered around Coral's and Gene's minds that evening. What was David doing last Friday until 1:30 A.M.? What was all that breath freshener doing on his dresser? Was he out that late with the guys or with the girls?

In the animal world, the young learn quickly how to be what they are. Within a relatively short time they are on their own, able to protect themselves reasonably well, gather food, establish shelter, and generally manage as adults of their particular species. Not so with humans. Not only does it take over two decades for a person to mature physically, but it takes at least as long to achieve moral, emotional, social, intellectual, and spiritual maturity. To top it off, when maturity is reached, integration seems to have only begun.

Achieving integration for the human is similar to the aging and mellowing process for wine. It simply takes time and the proper conditions for the soul to permeate the body, for the ever accumulating present to blend with the past, for experience to modulate principle, and for insight to deepen into wisdom.

Much of human life is a journey inward. Young love may start with external attraction, lead inward to the commitment of marriage, then further inward to the near fusion of souls in interpersonal communion. Relationships develop and personal ties strengthen, not by force of instinct, but by force of internalized values and deliberate choices.

A human being is never too old to learn; new information and fresh experiences are absorbed daily and integrated into what went before. Humans require a long time to "grow up" and a longer time to "grow in." Of the two, the inward journey is the more satisfying and fulfilling.

1. Integration is the dynamic process of becoming fully human, becoming whole.

The call to wholeness is the call to an integrated maturity. Maturity does not mean perfection, although it does mean the attainment of a certain degree of development. A whole person is one who has achieved a definite harmony of all essential elements in human life and experience. Each human being is called to wholeness. Our goal in life is to become the whole person, the integrated person, as conceived by God. A person cannot achieve integration without appropriately harmonizing genital sex into sexuality, and sexuality into one's total experience.

2. The term *sexuality* includes much more than genital sex.
All too often in today's world genitality is mistaken for sexuality, much as sex is mistaken for love. A distinction that may be helpful is that physical, biological sex is genital sex. Genital sex is not all of sexuality. The term *sexuality* is better understood if it includes all that it means to be male or female. Sexuality includes several dimensions—the physical, moral, social, spiritual, emotional and intellectual—combined with the appreciation of one's own sex (male or female) and also an appreciation of "the opposite sex." It is also necessary for a person to have the perspective that sex is only one aspect of sexuality.

3. Adolescents have the God-given task of integrating their sexuality consciously and deliberately.
The task of sexual integration is of special importance for the adolescent. During this time of growth God gives the young person the task of strengthening his or her sexual identity. This involves the acceptance of one's maleness or femaleness and the gradual affirmation of one's maleness or femaleness through lived experience. It is not unusual for young people to exaggerate their sexual identity as they learn its various dimensions and experiment with how those dimensions feel.

4. Temperance enables us to give proper direction to our movement toward sexual integration.
A virtue that directs our movement towards sexual integration is temperance. A basic objective reason for temperance is rooted in the dignity of the human person and the revelation that we

are temples of the Holy Spirit. A well-known youth catechist has advised high school teachers that the most important effect a religion teacher can have on youth is to help them realize, within themselves who they are as children of God, as temples of the Holy Spirit, and as members of the Body of Christ. If a teacher does this, the catechist contends, young people have been more than adequately served!

Overindulgence is the abuse of our bodies through the misuse of drink, drugs, smoking, eating, and sex. Youth today are very familiar with the phenomenon of overindulgence; they see it in many adults, and they see it very frequently among their peers. Temperance is the moral virtue which guides the urge or craving for what is pleasurable. Temperance always requires some degree of abstinence, that is, the keeping away from or controlling the use of some good. Temperance has to do with moderating a good. Drink is not evil in itself, nor is sex. It is the abuse of goods that is evil, and temperance concerns itself with the proper use of a good.

5. Chastity is that aspect of the virtue of temperance which regulates the use of the sexual powers.

Although some integration takes place unobtrusively and rather automatically, much occurs deliberately. The young male and female must integrate sex into their sexuality deliberately, as they must also consciously integrate their sexuality into the total person. One who consciously strives to integrate sexuality will find restraint and self-discipline to be an essential tool. It is difficult to imagine how, with the prevalence of the contraceptive mentality in our society, one could achieve integration without a great deal of deliberate discipline.

Also it is difficult to imagine integration happening without counsel. In this day of openness and explicitness about sexuality, the advice and counsel of prudent and well-integrated persons seems essential.

6. Some contemporary attitudes make the practice of chastity difficult.

The following list suggests some of the more prevalent attitudes that war against chastity:

a. Sex is a physical need similar to sleep or food and is thereby everyone's right.

b. Preoccupation with the techniques of love-making.

c. The illusion given by many movies and books that sex is the hero's reward after a difficult feat or dangerous episode.

d. "You only go around once" used as an invitation to license.

e. A person who does not have sex cannot be normal.

f. The double standard that sex is O.K. for males but not O.K. for females.

g. Sex is the solution to problems.

Often these attitudes are expressed indirectly and subtly. They manifest an unwholesome preoccupation with genital sex and destroy a well-balanced perspective on sex.

7. Vicarious experience is a principal means of integration or disintegration.

As young people, indeed people of all ages, strive to integrate their sexuality, they will find a great deal of challenge in vicarious experiences provided by books, movies, music, novels, and art. A vicarious experience is one felt or enjoyed through an imagined participation in the experience of others. With the daily intake of television, we are regularly influenced and affected, one way or another, through vicarious experiences. How does one integrate the vast amount of information that comes through the media? How does one achieve balance with the varied and even contradictory attitudes? How does a person bring it all together for good effect? Vicarious experiences can be disintegrating or integrating. We must learn to be directors of our own development.

8. In adolescence, relationships with others, God, and Church change, develop, and mature.

With the onset of puberty the young person experiences his or her sexuality in a very new and exciting way, more as an adult than as a child. The adolescent is a mixture of child and adult, capable of adult response with little children and capable of a childlike response with adults, especially parents. We marvel at the adultlike moments that young people manifest, just as we marvel at the childlike moments of adults. Affection, emotion, sexual feeling, sexual fears are experienced in a new and different way once puberty begins. Just as adults do not communicate with God as children do, so too, when teenagers become more adult they begin to communicate with God as adults communicate. We must, in St. Paul's words, "put away the things of a child" (I Corinthians 13:11).

It is important for teenagers to grow in their relationship with God in the same way that they grow in their relationships with people—more and more as adult to adult. Their prayers should change and develop as they become more capable of adult activity. Factors involved in adolescent growth and prayer are the deepened realization of mystery and the acceptance of mystery through internalized faith.

Also at this age conscience continues to develop and moral consciousness becomes more mature. Teenagers awaken to the significance of community in their lives. They develop a new and more adultlike social awareness. The place of tradition, customs, the role of law, all take on deeper meaning. Adolescents also develop a greater sense of history, seeing themselves much more naturally within the flow of history than they were able to do as children. Their sense of being one-in-the-many deepens; thus their greater appreciation for New Testament images of the Church, such as, the vine and the branches, the leaven in the dough, the building up of the Body of Christ, and "many members though one body" (I Corinthians 12:12).

Youth understand community better if they are encouraged or supported in starting projects, initiating friendships, and participating in community efforts. Christians need Church. Jesus established His religion as a community, people in communion with Himself and with each other, living the common life of the Spirit.

9. Youth need strong role models to give witness to moral strength.

Everyone needs and is touched by the example of others, but especially is this true of the young. The saying, "What you do speaks so loudly that I cannot hear what you say," is familiar to all.

Therefore, it is important for young people that teachers and parents and other significant adults give "loud" Christian witness. Also important are the lives of the saints as role models to help inspire and strengthen today's youth.

Of primary importance is belief in Jesus Christ as the Way, the Truth, and the Life. For the person who has committed his or her life to Jesus, following Christ means imitation of Christ. To follow Jesus Christ is to "put on the mind of Christ" and to imitate His example.

Over the centuries Mary, the Mother of Jesus, has been held in a position of special honor and esteem for her "Fiat" ("Let it be done according to Thy will") her "yes" to God, and for her life-long fidelity to her vocation. She has been called the "New Eve," the Mother of Jesus and of those united to Jesus through faith. Mary is honored as the Mother of the Church. Christians are encouraged to imitate her saintly life and to be drawn closer to Jesus and the Father through her example. Although Mary is often singled out for her chastity, she also possessed the other virtues to an admirable degree and deserves our attention and imitation.

LESSON 4   LIST OF TERMS

Balance

In reference to a life, putting all aspects of life into a harmonious whole.

Genitality

The biological, physical, reproductive dimension of sexuality, including pleasurable feelings. *Genitality* refers to physical experience of sex, including arousal and orgasm.

Integration

The process of making whole, bringing about a unity. A person is well-integrated when sexuality (including genital expression) is expressed in harmony with all the powers of the whole person.

Moderation

Deliberately tempering and shaping emotions and reactions toward pleasure and pain; establishing a balance; avoidance of extremes and excesses.

Overindulgence

To give in to a desire to an excessive degree, for example, to eating or drinking too much.

Preoccupation

Complete absorption of the mind with a particular interest to the exclusion of others.

Self-development

To fulfill one's capabilities; the direction of one's own life toward growth and maturity.

Self-restraint

To limit oneself; self-control; to hold oneself back.

Sexuality

That dimension of the person which makes a person male or female, capable of affective bonds and procreative activity.

Sin

Deliberate turning away from God.

Virtue

Habit of performing morally good actions.

Wholeness

Containing all the elements or parts; entire; complete.

5 Self-Esteem and Intimacy

Debbie believed deep down that if Tom really knew her, he wouldn't like her. This wasn't a new feeling in her life. She was told even when a child that she was "less than average" and not very attractive. Teased at home by two older brothers, she endured more teasing at school after a teacher dubbed her the "sphinx." Her size had been a terrible burden to her, but she was growing in self-esteem primarily because she was good at handcrafts and painting.

She and Tom had been good friends now for nearly two years. They saw each other twice a week on the average. Their most serious conversations focused on his plans for college. Rarely did they ever come close to topics of a more personal nature. Neither was encouraged at home to talk about feelings. Living in a very conservative, lower middle-class neighborhood, their school curriculum and environment practically denied the emotional aspects of life.

Once, on a parish-sponsored retreat which both had attended, the leaders asked everyone to share something personal. Debbie had planned to describe the good feelings she had when Tom complimented her on her craftwork, but she got cold feet and just talked about how disappointed she was that it was raining. The girl who spoke after Debbie got emotional as she told about her friend's seeking advice from her about having an abortion. Tom felt embarrassed that anyone should even mention such a thing on a retreat. Even so, he wished he felt secure enought about himself to be more expressive and share what he truly felt. Maybe some day, he would be able to, but not yet. Instead he took the easy way out, excusing himself when his turn came, saying that he didn't feel well.

The over-forty generations remember when talk about self-love was denounced as selfish and not Christian. You were not supposed to take much pride (although a little was allowed in some circles!) in your accomplishments. You were not encouraged to build yourself up, lest you think too highly of yourself.

Today, the emphasis is in the other direction. Human potential programs, assertiveness workshops, affirmation seminars, books and magazines promoting self-growth and self-esteem—all these and more are efforts to pump greater degrees of positive feelings towards self into millions of people.

Low self-esteem is a serious problem for many people. Few doubt that it is a major factor in teenage prostitution, drug use, and the high suicide rate. It is often the villain in marriage failures and relational conflicts. Failure in school or work, loneliness, depression, physical illness, and other troubles can frequently be traced to low self-value.

Many patterns of how people relate to family and friends are rooted in how they relate to themselves. It is doubtful that a person who hates him- or herself is able to love anyone else. Christian tradition has a powerful message about love of self. The Gospel calls for self-love. Jesus stated the great commandments in these terms, "Love your neighbor as you love yourself."

Developing a healthy love of self is not an easy task for most people—and it is very difficult for some. Our society is quick to label and stereotype, abuse and oppress, those who fail to conform to majority standards. People who are treated in these manners usually find it extremely difficult to develop positive feelings about themselves. Treated as of little value by others, they come to believe it of themselves.

Such is the situation of many homosexuals in our society. Indeed, a particular difficulty within the Christian community in our times is the question of how the Church is to respond to homosexuals. The topic cannot and should not be avoided. The Church is attempting to respond compassionately and intelligently to homosexuals, as it tries also to remain faithful to its teaching responsibility. The problem of low self-esteem relates directly to the homosexual's experience, as it does to the lived experience of so many others in our society.

The principles which follow provide a foundation for education in self-worth and sexuality:

1. Christian tradition holds to the basic goodness of all creation, including every human being.
The creation stories in the book of Genesis reveal that humanity was made in God's image, "male and female he created them." God looked at everything that He had made and He found it very good. Later in the Wisdom literature, Scripture states that "God formed man to be imperishable; the image of His own nature He made Him." Psalm 8 says "What is man that you should care for him? You have made him little less than the angels, and crowned him with glory and honor. You have given him rule over the works of your hands, putting all things under his feet."

If we would look at ourselves with the eyes of God, we would see how valued and valuable we are. St. Paul in his first letter to the Corinthians says, "You must know that your body is a temple of the Holy Spirit, who is within—the spirit you have received from God. You are not your own. You have been purchased, and at a price. So glorify God in your body" (1 Corinthians 6:19–20). Christian tradition has been constant in teaching the tremendous value of the human person, blessed as it is with the promise of bodily resurrection.

2. We believe we are made in the image and likeness of God.
Each person is a unique creation of God, reflecting in his or her own manner some aspect of the Divine. Vatican II's Constitution on the Church in the Modern World teaches us about the dignity of the human person. Human persons are immortal. "Thus, when he recognizes in himself a spiritual and immortal soul, he is not being mocked by a fantasy born only of physical or social influences, but is rather laying hold of the proper truth of the matter" (no. 14).

Human persons are to be valued because of what they are, not primarily because of what they do. Self-worth can be based on either or both of two factors, namely, *being* and *doing*. So often today self-esteem is based on one's usefulness and one's "market value." People are taught to measure their worth by what they accomplish, that is, by what they do and achieve. Is there not a more basic value prior to this? The Christian view holds that a person's essential worth comes more from being than doing.

The infant, the blind and crippled, the mentally retarded, the feeble—each person has an inherent worth as a human being, a worth that does not have to be earned or merited. Neither is this worth lost or diminished by mistakes or sin or other types of failure. Self-esteem is the value with which one holds himself or herself. It is a person's sense of worth, the feeling and knowledge of self-worth. It is the valuing of one's self and the consequent reverencing of one's self that this valuing calls forth.

3. Self-worth is greatly dependent upon establishing sexual identity.
Psychologists tell us that sexual identity is fairly well established by age four or five. They also claim that a person's basic sense of self-esteem is determined in these earliest years. Unfortunately, our society manages to convey and maintain sexual stereotypes and sexist attitudes. Often these are associated with

sexual roles; for example, only men can be carpenters and women, nurses. Certainly, some differences do exist between men and women, by nature, and some roles (probably few in number) may require one sex rather than the other. But such roles would seem to be few. Most jobs, roles, and responsibilities need to be done by people.

Without being overly sensitive, Christians need to be aware of sex role stereotyping and sexist language. St. Paul wrote "There is neither male nor female, Jew nor Greek, slave nor free . . ." (Galatians 3:28). Under God, we are all equal and we are called to be brothers and sisters to one another. Children learn when very young the attitudes of their elders about being male or female. Any derisiveness, name-calling, or other actions which "put-down" either sex should have no place in the Christian community.

4. A major contemporary concern is the homosexual's struggle for personal integrity and dignity.
Still very deep-seated in our society is prejudicial treatment and bias towards lesbians (female homosexuals) and gay men. The Church's commitment to promote and protect the human dignity and human rights of every person, including homosexuals, will cause conflict and anger in those who dislike or even hate persons claiming to have homosexual orientations. Even so, their basic dignity and rights cannot be denied them. Catholic homosexuals have a right to just treatment from the Church the same as anyone else. This much lesbians and gays can insist upon and expect from their Church.

What they cannot expect is a retraction by the Church of its moral stand on homosexual activity. Because Church teaching holds to an inseparable link between the unitive and procreative purposes in sexual activity, sexual acts between homosexuals are not morally good, since such acts cannot possibly be procreative. A distinction is made between homosexual orientation (which is not immoral) and homosexual activity (which is immoral). Homosexual orientation is a predominant tendency one has to be sexually attracted to persons of the same sex. A person may have an homosexual orientation but refrain from homosexual activity.

5. The Church recognizes that not everything is known about homosexuality.

Whatever psychology, anthropology, and other sciences can unearth in order to increase our understanding of homosexuality is certainly welcomed. Many today believe that homosexuality is "just as normal as heterosexuality," and their argument is based upon the idea that at least some homosexuals seem to be homosexual from birth. The argument goes that since they are born this way, it must be natural. They claim that the centuries of abuse and degradation that homosexuals have endured represent a "dark age" mentality. They feel that a more enlightened age, such as our own, will overcome the darkness and recognize the "normalcy" of this particular sexual orientation. This assessment, the Church holds, is erroneous.

This is not to say that the Church does not wish to promote greater understanding of the homosexual person. Some Catholic homosexuals and advocates of gays have formed into a group known as Dignity. Their hope is not only to raise the consciousness of Catholics about the gay condition and the prejudice that gays experience, but also to legitimize homosexuality within the Church. However, the United States Bishops have taken a clear and strong stand that homosexual activity is morally wrong since it denies the procreative function of sex.

6. Every person seeks intimacy in personal relationships.

Intimacy is often understood to mean sexual closeness involving genital activity. However, it can and does mean much more. Two persons can be intimate without being sexually active, and, vice versa, two persons can be sexually active and not be intimate. Intimacy is essentially a quality of soul and heart. It exists when people share their personal selves, when their hearts meet in a close personal relationship.

44

It is generally recognized that every person has a need for genuine intimacy. Created to be social beings, people require other people, not just to be present bodily or physically, as in a crowd, but to be present personally, as in friendship.

Genuine intimacy with another is experienced by most people, it seems; although everybody apparently has to work at maintaining it. Intimacy is not always easily won or accomplished. Requiring attention and occasionally caution, intimacy is earned to a great extent. Personal relationships which are characterized by intimacy are built up gradually, with plenty of care and by deliberate injections of love. They withstand some pain and demand some sacrifice; they require risk-taking and persistent efforts at unconditional love. Forgiveness is a part of intimacy's progress.

Because intimacy is often confused with sexual activity, youth need to know the distinctions between the two. They will appreciate guidance which leads them to the formation of genuine intimate relationships, including an appreciation of the distinction between sex and intimacy, as well as their relationship.

7. Self-esteem can be enhanced through acceptance and love.
When someone shares a secret with us we feel privileged and worthwhile, accepted for who we are. When people close to us share their deepest values, convictions, struggles, and joys, we feel worthwhile. Parents and teachers who entrust themselves in confident ways to young people encourage them to cherish and value their own selves. Valued by others, they have more reason to value themselves.

Adults responsible for children and youth can make the mistake of failing to affirm and accept the goodness and accomplishments of youth. Feeling the need to motivate the young, adults sometimes over-emphasize possibility and underestimate reality. Bishop Fulton Sheen used to suggest that children be patted on the back low enough and hard enough, recommending in his gentle teasing way that parents need not fear spanking a child if it helps growth toward the good and right. In light of the great hesitancy many adults have today for affirming their children, I would suggest a variation to the Bishop's theme: children need to be patted on the back high enough and low enough, and the proper amount in both places. Affirmation, compliments, recognition of the good, valuing the efforts they make—all these are very important for the young. (In fact, they are equally important for adults.) Everybody needs to be recognized and affirmed for the good they are and do.

8. Experimentation is often used in the development of one's sexual identity and sense of self-worth.

Little girls like to play house and wear their mother's shoes. Little boys like to imitate Dad in the male role. Sometimes children switch and try on the role of the opposite sex, just to see what it feels like. Later on, as adolescents, young men and women continue to experiment with sexual roles and identity. What does it feel like to be a woman, a man? How does it feel for me to be a woman or a man?

With the rapid change of physical appearance during adolescence, youth find themselves struggling almost daily with understanding and accepting their sexual identity. It is a natural thing for them to "try on" their identity by experimentation.

9. Youth can benefit greatly from the counsel and encouragement of adults.

While they grow into and through adolescence toward a wholesome and healthy self-acceptance and identity, young people need adults who can share honestly with them their perspectives and advice on personal development. Adults do have something to give that youth do not yet have, and that is knowledge that only experience brings. The inexperienced can learn much from the experienced.

Not that experience is the only teacher, or even the best in all instances; but if the young will listen to the experience of others, they can avoid much damage and harm to themselves and others . Every now and then a person will claim that "unless you've experienced it, you'll never know." Many things in life can be assessed from another's experience. We can and do learn from others. Especially is this important when we are talking about damaging and hurtful experiences.

Young people who believe in the philosophy that experience is the only teacher would benefit from a serious reflection on the positive advantages of learning from the mistakes and wisdom of others.

LESSON 5   LIST OF TERMS

Esteem	High regard, value, worth; to hold in great respect and admiration.
Gay	Term usually used to designate a male homosexual person. Can also designate female.
Heterosexuality	Manifestation of sexual attraction for persons of the opposite sex.
Homosexuality	Manifestation of sexual attraction for persons of the same sex.
Homosexual Activity	Attempt at sexual intercourse and/or sexual intimacy between persons of the same sex.
Homosexual Orientation	Sexual attraction toward persons of the same sex.
Human Dignity	Worthiness as a human being; basic God-given value and worth.
Human Rights	That which is due to a person because he or she is a human being; basic claims coming from one's nature, such as the right to life, pursuit of human fulfillment, right to worship, to be regarded as a human being, etc.
Intimacy	Closeness between persons; warm, loving friendship, often characterized by signs of affection; sharing of deepest selves.
Lesbian	Term commonly used to designate the female homosexual person.
Self-acceptance	Approval of oneself; acceptance of self by oneself.
Self-image	One's conception of oneself or of one's role.
Self-respect	Reverence for oneself as a human being.
Self-worth	Personal value; self-esteem.

6 Challenges to Integration

Randy ran with a fast crowd. Flooded with four-letter words and sexual innuendos, their talk would make a construction worker blush. Once, while Randy was replacing a set of bearings on his junker, his mom overheard him describe to his buddy his imagined sexual explorations and conquests with a girlfriend. Disappointed that he would be thinking that way, his mother found a time later that day to express her hope that he would always treat women with respect.

Angered that she had heard the earlier conversation and feeling that it was none of her business, Randy hopped into his car and sped to his favorite hangout on Park Avenue, overlooking the river bluff. Here, at least, he would not be hassled. Maybe the guys would show up and they would do something interesting for the evening.

No one was occupying the near-horizontal tree trunk he liked to straddle. Grabbing a "girlie" magazine he had stored in his glove compartment, he made his way along the trunk, perched himself at the fork, leafed through the magazine, and let his mind drift.

He loved to escape into this sexual world. Here, he could be master of his relationships. No one spoiled his desires. True, there were limits to what his mind could do, but no limits to what his mind could imagine. Tenderness would mix itself with violence. Was this love or lust? Did he enjoy

*the violence more than the tenderness? He didn't know or
really care. He was away from Mom and her constant
prying, secure, at least for the moment, in his own thoughts.*

Adolescence can be a time of confusion and intense emotion.
It is as though the young person held the reins to a dozen
horses, each trying to rush off in a direction separate from the
others. How do you get them to pull in unison in the same
direction? How does a person establish and maintain control
over his or her life in all its dimensions?

Sexual awakening, beginning with puberty, ushers the child
into a period of a decade or so of extremely important development. Drawn by the charm and wit of other teens, themselves
budding sexually, the young feel the excitement of romance
and infatuation, friendship and gang closeness, freedom, and
independence. Balance and moderation are not the hallmark
of youth. Rather, the young tend toward excess, imbalance,
and immoderation. They will stay up too late, party too long,
drink too much, drive too fast, play too hard, eat too irregularly,
and commit themselves to causes without thorough investiga-
tion. For many, moderation is dull and balance is boring. They
prefer the excitement of living at the extreme.

In a society which extols pleasure and immediate gratification, the responsibility which parents and teachers have of
teaching moderation, restraint, and self-discipline to youth is
probably more difficult to carry out—but no less important.

The movies teens see, the songs they listen to, the heroes and
heroines they admire most often promote casual and matter-
of-fact attitudes towards sex. While this situation may have
the advantage of bringing sex "out into the open," thereby
making it easier for parents to discuss, the disadvantage is the
disintegration that it encourages. We human beings are called
to wholeness and integration.

1. The process of integration is life-long.
Integration is a dynamic process in which a human becomes more developed and complete. The process is never finished, even in a lifetime. Children are challenged to grow in a balanced way, youth are challenged, so are adults. Even in old age a person can grow more complete and attain a greater personal harmony. In a sentence, the human being is called to continually grow towards the wholeness that God has conceived. Humans are very complex creatures. One part or another can get partially or completely out of control, and the result is imbalance. The need to restore balance and harmony is a constant life-long need.

2. Meeting the challenges to integration directly can strengthen moral character.
Integration will not occur unless one practices, that is, actualizes integration. We learn by doing. Acting rightly and doing good deeds can actually help one become right and good. In a sense, we can grow into our good deeds. For example, one grows in honesty by being honest. Recognizing imbalances and restoring balance, recognizing disharmony and restoring harmony, recognizing inadequate understanding and learning more are examples of the dynamic process of integration.

3. Sexual fears can be either integrating or disintegrating.
Sexual fears are emotional responses that arise from anxiety or worry about sexual thought or action. Such anxieties are a common experience and happen to some degree or another in everyone's life. They are neither good nor bad in themselves, their morality depending on what a person chooses to do with them. Some sexual fears are helpful in that they guide us in the avoidance of something that may cause harm to us. It is a good thing, for example, to be afraid of some realities, such as, seductive persons or hitchhiking. The reasonable fear that one is not developing sexually in a normal way will lead that person to see a doctor. These fears are healthy and helpful.

There is another kind of sexual fear that is not healthy, however. The person who worries that he or she is sterile or impotent without any medical, factual reason has an unfounded and unreasonable anxiety. Worry about physical appearance, or preoccupation about things that can't be changed, do not contribute to positive growth. Fears can get so burdensome that they may control a person rather than the person controlling them.

4. Sexual fantasies can be either integrating or disintegrating. A sexual fantasy is an imagined sequence which is sexual in content, a kind of homemade private movie made and seen in one's own head. Fantasies can be helpful or harmful to growth; they can be wholesome or unwholesome. Some fantasies will assist a person in sorting out values, in making decisions about what he or she should do. God gave us an imagination for a purpose; but like other faculties and powers, imagination can be abused and misused. Young people should know that sexual arousal usually begins in the brain, starting with the imagination. They should be discouraged from allowing their imaginations to go uncontrolled, especially with regard to sexual content. They should be encouraged to discipline their minds and to control their thoughts. Deliberate sexual fantasies, as unchaste thoughts, can be sinful in themselves, before one acts them out.

If people dwell in their imagination on cheating or shoplifting, if they fantasize about the thrill and challenge of these activities, they may convince themselves to go out and more easily do the immoral activity. Books, magazines, movies, and even legitimate material which treat sexual subjects may serve to stimulate sexual activity in unhealthy and immoral ways. Young people understand air pollution and the effect that polluted air has on physical health. They can also understand moral pollution and the effect unwholesome material has on moral health and moral environment.

5. The ready availability of pornographic material calls for moral judgment almost on a daily basis.
Pornography is obscene literature, art, or photography. It lacks artistic value, offends decency, and is intended to arouse lust and sexual excitement. Pornographic material uses the person for something other than a good and moral purpose, simply as an object or commodity.

Our society has experienced a breakdown in the protective codes surrounding sexuality. Stores, air terminals, barber shops, and even many homes today have pornographic material which is readily available to children and youth. The increased use of vulgar language on TV, in the media, and in daily conversation, manifests a more lax attitude towards sex. The bumper sticker morality and the double "entendre" manifests that substantial changes have occurred in sexual mores since the 1950s.

It should be recognized by teachers and parents that there can be a certain relativity in this matter. People can become "immune" to certain kinds of exposure. For example, someone unaccustomed to vulgar language may be shocked and even disturbed when first exposed to it. After a certain amount of exposure he or she may have adjusted and at this point find little or even no difficulty. All this is to say that though things may be, in fact, not pornographic to one person, they can be pornographic to another. The adult has the responsibility to be a censor for himself or herself. Because children and adolescents are still being shaped and developed, attempts to debase the minds of the young with pornographic material are especially reprehensible.

6. Greater understanding about masturbation provides helpful insights on how it affects the process of integration.
Integration is the process of becoming whole and fulfilled. Masturbation, which is defined as the handling of one's own genitals for the purpose of sexual self-gratification, can have negative

effects on sexual integration. Traditional Church teaching holds that masturbation is sinful because of the self-centeredness of the act, and because sexual powers are meant to be used for the procreation of children and the strengthening of the love between husband and wife. If sex is given to us for purposes that essentially are other-directed, turning inward may be less than integrating.

7. Not everything is known about masturbation; however, the insights of psychologists and mental health personnel are contributing to a better understanding.
Researchers point out that although sexual pleasure is the reason behind much masturbation, often reasons other than sexual pleasure are present. Masturbation may be done to release emotional and/or physical tension, to escape from the threat of a difficult reality, or to serve as a substitute for real and genuine intimacy. The reasons, in these instances, are not wholly sexual. Some psychologists suggest that in such situations masturbation may be a sign that something else in one's life needs attention. The real problem may not be sexual at all. Confessors who have counseled persons with a habit of masturbation realize the complexity involved and the difficulty in sorting out the essential factors.

8. In its pastoral care of young people who experience masturbation, the Church advises the following guidelines.
First, avoid the extremes—the one extreme which sees masturbation as something "normal" and not having any moral content at all, and the other extreme which sees it as totally degrading and morally reprehensible. The truth lies somewhere in the middle. Masturbation is considered to be a challenge to a wholly integrated sexuality, a challenge that is commonly experienced and commonly mastered. Excessive worry and guilt are to be avoided, as is a totally lax and carefree attitude.

Second, the Church's teaching on masturbation should be presented to young people in the context of the total picture of sexuality and the call to wholeness. As with other moral choices, this one, too, necessitates a recognition of the power of prayer and sacraments in living up to the ideals of the Christian life. In adolescence, when sexual development is especially intense and complex, the problem of masturbation tends to be more prevalent. As young people struggle with integration in other areas, such as honesty, respect for property and person, relationship to God, personal authenticity, and mature relationships with their parents, so also their struggle with sexual integration is a necessary part of life.

9. The call to wholeness is God-given, and one that we can respond to only partially in this life.
Perfection, total integration, is not something we achieve this side of heaven. Still, we are called toward it; we are invited to choose the way to it. Strong in Christian tradition is the belief that human beings always choose what they perceive to be good. Though we may realize later that our perceptions were wrong, either because of misinformation, lack of information, emotional blindness, or some other reason, our choices were made because of some good desired.

Wholeness is a good we can choose. What's more, having chosen this good, lots of other choices will be made in the light of it. Youth can know that wholeness and integration are desirable. They can choose wholeness, and they can make other choices in the light of it.

LIST OF TERMS

Compulsion	Irresistible impulse to do something one does not want to do.
Impotence	Complete failure of the sexual power, especially in the male; incapability of performing sexual intercourse.
Integration	Process of making whole, bringing about a unity. A person is well-integrated when sexuality (including genital expression) is expressed in harmony with all the powers of the whole person.
Lust	Uncontrolled and illicit sexual desire, usually toward another person.
Masturbation	Manipulation of one's own genitals for the purpose of self-gratification.
Obscenity	Something offensive to decency or modesty; for example, language or literature that offends community standards.
Pornography	Material that depicts obscene behavior and is intended to cause sexual excitement.
Preoccupation	Complete absorption of the mind or interests to the point of distraction from the ordinary affairs of life.
Sexual Fantasy	Imagined sequence which is sexual in content; a kind of home-made private film, made and seen within one's own imagination.
Sexual Fear	Emotional response that arises from anxiety or worry about a sexual thought or action.
Sterility	The state of being incapable of having children; barren; unfruitful; incapable of producing offspring.
Temperance	Virtue that directs one's movements towards integration; self-restraint in the seeking of pleasure.

7 Responsibility for Relationships

Jodie slammed her bedroom door, flung herself on her bed, and wept fitfully. Her parents had just told her of their disappointment in her choice of friends, particularly, Jeff, her boyfriend. What right did they have to determine her personal relationships, she questioned.

Jodie's parents saw it differently. They believed that Jodie had fallen "head over heels" in love with a very attractive man six years her senior. At fifteen and experiencing her "first love," Jodie seemed to have totally lost control of her life. Thoughts of Jeff consumed her time, energy, and interest. Teachers complained that her work had become shoddy and inconsistent. At home, she nearly burned the house down the night before through carelessness and preoccupation. No wonder her parents were concerned. Cindy, her best girlfriend, was also becoming concerned. Jodie had so little time for her now.

Tomorrow Jodie would open her heart to Mrs. Johnson, her favorite teacher and her running coach. Thay had become good friends. Jodie could tell "Mrs J." everything. They would talk about her relationship with Jeff, her anger over her parents' rejection of Jeff, and her thoughts of running away from home. Mrs. J. would help Jodie understand. At least she would give it a good try.

It was going to be difficult. Jodie felt awfully grown up for her age. Although her parents didn't nag, she was decidedly more self-determined than Cindy and had been making her own decisions about her life for some time now. She believed she was on top of the situation. It would take a miracle to convince her otherwise!

The dictionary defines relationship as "the connection, emotional or otherwise, between people." Obviously, things can also be in relationship to each other; for example, a rock to a tree, a car to a house. Relationships between things are a very different matter from relationships between people. Relationships between people are personal. They involve the mind, heart, intellect, and will of individual persons in relationship to each other.

Adolescents experience tremendous changes in their personal relationships. For example, a kiss is a sign of affection, but it may also be a sign of one person's desire for sexual intimacy with another. A boy who is seven years old may be kissed by a girl who is seven. The same sign of affection seven years later when the child has become an adolescent may mean something quite different. Personal relationships for adolescents developing their adult sexual capacities bring a whole new dimension of experience to their lives. Talking with, being with, and sharing with members of the opposite sex can be a new and exciting experience, one that is very important in the normal development of sexual identity and the capacity for heterosexual relationships.

In many ways adolescents experience a new birth. As the infant learns to walk (be mobile and get around) and talk (communicate one's self) in the world, so in adolescence a person must learn to get around and to communicate in the new world of adult personal relationships. In adolescence these relationships have the potential of being explicitly sexual.

Sexuality is awakened even between members of the same sex. Young men must learn how to show affection to other men without fear of homosexuality and without anxiety over the appropriateness of this kind of expression. The same is true with young women. Needless to say it is very important that young men and young women feel at home with their own sexual identity and feel comfortable being themselves with persons of the same or opposite sex.

1. In adolescence, relationships tend to become more sexual.
In early adolescence the boy begins to experience himself not so much as a child, but more as a man, and the girl more as a woman. With increased sexual development they begin to realize the possibility of their being parents someday, the possibility of their bearing children, and having a loving and sexual relationship. They now realize from the inside what it means or could mean to be "sexy." All of this and more awakens at this age. Sexuality becomes more intimately intertwined with relationships. A person comes to taste a new kind of happiness and fulfillment, the kind that can come through fulfilling and wholesome personal relationships.

2. In adolescence, relationships also tend to become more responsible.
Adolescents realize more deeply that they are capable of being responsible persons, that is, they have the capacity for moral decision making and, therefore, are accountable to someone or some order beyond and outside themselves. One thing responsibility certainly means is accountability; a person is answerable to someone beyond self.

Our sexuality was given to us as a gift from God our Creator. We are expected to use it responsibly, and we will be held accountable according to our Creator's expectations. Finally, we will be asked to account for what He has given us, and we will then be praised or chastised as we deserve.

3. Most teenagers have relationships with family, school, peer group and Church.

Since most teens live at home with their parents and their families, their experiences of personal relationships are still very much family-centered. Most of them will have daily contact with their parent or parents, their brothers and sisters. Despite the great amount of mobility in today's society, most teenagers will have some relationship with their extended families—grandparents, uncles, aunts, cousins, and others. Even if their only contact is by mail, they will usually feel a kinship or blood relationship to those special people in their lives.

Also very important to the teenager are the relationships established at school. Teachers, deans, counselors, coaches, nurses, cooks, librarians, teacher aides and others will play a major or minor role in the students' lives. Those who play a major role in a young person's life are truly "significant others" and can have a profound and deep influence on their futures. Also significant for teenagers are their peer relationships, relationships they have with people their own age. These can range from merely physical, for example, sitting in the same class together, to very deep personal relationships, such as, friendship.

Youth with a religious background and involvement also will identify relationships which have grown out of their faith community. They know and relate to other worshipers, clergy, youth ministers, and parish personnel. Their faith community can support and reinforce family values, sometimes even serving as a substitute home for young people whose families are in disarray or scattered geographically.

Experience is unquestionably a most effective teacher. Central to a person's interpretation of experience is the person's philosophy of life. Obviously if a person believes that people are evil and never can be trusted, this belief will color every interpretation of the human experience. If, on the other hand, one believes that people are basically good, and that sometimes a person can act in an evil, manipulative, or cruel manner, this interpretation will give another kind of meaning to experience. It is important for the young person to realize that he or she is good but that even good people at times will do cruel, manipulative, or evil things.

Youth need to be encouraged to listen to their own experience, and to learn about themselves. They must examine and assess their experience. If they are being exploited or are exploiting someone else, they ought to be able to recognize it and to identify it for what it is. Adults can encourage youth to identify their experiences and be deliberate in their responses.

4. Youth learn the requirements of friendship.

True friendship has three characteristics. First, it requires union of one person with another. Often this union begins with admiration. You see something in the other person that you like and admire. This leads to your placing trust and hope in that person, and loving that person for himself or herself. Friendship requires unity of hearts.

Secondly, friendship requires that each promotes the good of the other. You want what is good and helpful for your friend. Genuine relationships are associations between people which are founded on something worthwhile and which help to promote the good of the other. A friendship must have the good of the other as a goal and as an intended outcome. True friendship cannot exist if evil or harm is intended.

Third, friendship requires reciprocity. You do not demand that your friend be good to you; you hope for it, but it must be returned freely. Friendship does not exist, in fact, until it is returned freely. You can "be a friend" to another but a friendship does not exist until the other becomes a friend to you. It should be noted that "being a friend" to another is a good thing, even when the other does not return the friendship. You can hope for the return; you cannot force it.

Adolescence is a very important time to learn deeper meanings of friendship. Children have friends. When they grow up to be adolescents, their capacity for friendship deepens and their experience of friendship changes. In adolescence they learn that friendship involves a lot of give and take, the sharing of some common interests, and mutual trusting. Adolescents have more to entrust to another person, thus the amount of risk they place in entrusting themselves and their secrets to another is much greater than when they were children. Teenage is a very important time for growth in friendship.

5. Youth may experience exploitative relationships and can learn from them.
Terms such as "fair-weather friend" and "foul-weather friend" indicate to a person a truth about friendship. Teenagers should examine their own relationships and friendships in the light of these or other helpful phrases. A friend loves his or her friend for himself or herself, not for what he or she can give. A relationship is exploitative when one person uses another person as an object, quite often for one's own enjoyment or personal gain. The motivation is selfish. One takes from another without giving. Sex is a common area in which people exploit people. A very vivid and awful example of exploitation is rape. In rape, someone uses another strictly for exploitative purposes. Respect and reverence for the person is defiled. It is also a helpful thing to see and understand rape as an act of violence, even more than as an act of sex.

Our Christian tradition strongly urges us to treat other people as we would want them to treat us. No one should like being manipulated or used by another. Teenagers can understand what this means and they should be encouraged to take a very strong stand against exploitative relationships, manipulative relationships, and relationships which do not respect or reverence the person of the other.

6. Infatuation is often a stage of learning to love, but it is not enough to get married on!

Infatuation has been called "foolish love," love in which one person feels possessed by or feels in possession of another person with a kind of foolish passion. Infatuated persons may be more in love with love than they are with each other. There is something unreal about the relationship. Captivated by a false image of another or in love with a projected image of a person, the infatuated lover is in love with a dream. When he or she awakes from the dream, little remains but a vague memory.

7. Young people can experience committed love and develop their own capacity for it.

Committed love is the free choice to oblige oneself to another. Committed love may or may not involve and include friendship. People may be committed to each other though they may not be friends. A mother or father is committed to an infant, but they are not necessarily friends. A child may be committed to his or her parents when the parents become old, but they may or may not have a friend relationship. The same is possible for a married couple. Some marriages have committed love but not necessarily friendship between the spouses. They may be committed to fidelity and permanence and children but their marriage relationship is not conditioned upon friendship. It will be obvious that a marriage where there is friendship along with commitment is a true blessing indeed. Friendship within marriage has a high value for many, if not most, people in our society.

8. Youth who are naive, overexposed, or pseudo-sophisticated can benefit from caring and honest adults.

Simplicity may be a virtue but if it means naiveté, it is not virtuous. A naive person is one who lacks experience, judgment, or information. Such a person is "out of touch" with reality and is very vulnerable. Naive persons are vulnerable beyond reason. Though our purpose is not to scare teenagers needlessly, nor exaggerate the dangers that life holds, neither is it to withhold from them the facts they need to live in the real world. Some people are more naive than others, and perhaps some are even just naturally naive. Lacking a realistic sense, having poor judgment, and being quite limited in experience, some people simply are uninformed and unaware of things they should be knowledgeable about. This is one extreme.

At the other extreme is overexposure. Already at a very tender age some young people have been subjected to "adult" experiences. Their home environments leave much to be desired. Parental fighting, husband battering, wife battering, child beating, incest, pornography, and profuse vulgarity are the experiences of many children and youth. Also, young people today have a great deal more exposure to adult experiences through the media, especially television, and some youth experience peer environments at school or in their neighborhood which are very unwholesome.

Genuine sophistication takes a great deal of experience and time. Some youth suffer from a false sophistication, pretending or believing they have more knowledge and awareness than they actually do. In some ways this attempt to appear "in control," when in reality they may not be, is normal. Since the adolescent world is so often turned upside down, adults could expect that occasionally the adolescent would enjoy the feeling of being in touch with the ground even if this means to pretend. This false sense of maturity may express itself in these phrases: "We have had all this stuff before." "We know all this material." "Gee, are you ever behind the times."

It can also show up in the teenager's use of language without understanding what the language means. Sometimes when challenged, they will refuse to explain themselves, laying upon their parents or teacher the label of "you're really out of it." Another common tactic is for the teenager to distract the attention of the teacher or parent away from himself or herself and draw the attention to someone else or some other topic. Such teenagers need firm and strong direction from adults. Parents and teachers must maintain confidence in themselves and find ways to move these pseudo-sophisticates to face reality, learn the facts, and effectively search for meaning.

9. Youth can develop the skill of examining and naming their relational experiences.

Every individual person experiences relationships in a different way from everyone else. Persons are unique. No two people live alike, share alike, love alike, forgive, trust, hope or confide in exactly the same way. No two persons assert their independence or manifest their dependence in exactly the same way. Obviously teachers and parents must remember the uniqueness and individuality of each person when they attempt to help young people grow.

Despite our individuality, we do experience many things in common. Every person experiences relationships and almost every person experiences exploitative relations, infatuation, and friendship. Even though we may experience the same kind of relationships, our individual experience is unlike another's experience. Each relationship is unique.

Being able to examine and name our relationships helps us live in the real world and develop our capacity for genuine fulfilling friendship and committed love.

LIST OF TERMS

Affection
Fondness toward another; emotional part of a person's love toward another; feelings of devotion toward another; any tender attachment.

Commitment
Decisive moral choice that involves a person in a definite course of action; conviction toward someone or something, accompanied by giving one's word.

Covenant Love
Formal, solemn, and binding union; a relationship initiated by God and calling for a faith response from the people; freely given, faithful, and permanent.

Exploitation
Unjust or improper use of another person for one's own profit or advantage; taking from another without giving; abuse of friendship.

Friendship
A relationship that seeks the welfare of another; a give-and-take relationship; mutual respect and loyalty built upon common interests.

Infatuation
Strong and unreasoning attachment; "in love" with love; the state of being blindly in love.

Personal Relationship
Relationship between people, involving the mind and heart of persons in relationship to each other.

Responsibility
Accountability for one's actions; capable of moral decisions and, therefore, accountable for one's acts.

Sacrificial Love
Giving without receiving; examples: parental love, married love, child taking care of older parents.

Unconditional Love
To be for another person without restriction; loving another without setting any limits; loving without placing conditions; being generous when no return is expected; being for another person even when the other can't return the love; loving without counting the cost.

8 Learning to Socialize

Skip spent most summer evenings at the pavilion. That's where the action was. The guys typically pulled their vans, cars, and cycles into the parking lot, hauled out their varied beverages, and settled down for the first phase of the evening's activities, the "peacock stage." Time to strut and show your stuff, maybe make a pass or two at some girl, maybe play hard to get. Almost everybody knew the ritual and the rules; the regulars could smell a novice a mile away.

That's what Cheryl was the evening she caught Skip's attention—a novice—her first time at the pavilion. She and Skip had known each other from school and had felt a special respect and care for each other. When their eyes met, they both felt slightly embarrassed at being seen at the pavilion's mating game. Anxious that Cheryl not be picked up by any guy "on the make," Skip called her over and invited her to go get a pizza with him. Grateful for the opportunity to be with him, and happy to leave the wolf-whistles and glances of the city's "finest" boys, Cheryl accepted.

When they returned two hours later, the situation looked much as they had left it, except that the music was louder, the beer flowed more freely, and the cars cruising were lined up bumper to bumper. Skip and Cheryl sat on the edge of the group and continued the conversation begun over pizza. They caught some of the obscene, sexist remarks made by the guys who pulled their van next to Skip's. In this environment people soon learned to listen to what others said but to be cautious about their own reaction. A language and symbol system existed here that carried significance only for the initiated. Cheryl felt some distance from it all, but safe now in a relationship which she was beginning to trust.

In the 1950s teenagers followed the fads of the day in clothing styles, hair styles, popular music, dances, and leisure activities, but nobody called it a subculture. Possibly because it wasn't. Teens still had strong ties to their families and churches. School was their opportunity to get an education. If they had jobs and some independent and personal income, they usually spent it on essentials or saved up for college.

Many things are different for today's teens. They have at their disposal greater amounts of undesignated monies than any generation of youth before them. Some save for college, some spend it on clothes, food, and basic living. Most goes for recreation and nonessentials: records, tapes, electronic equipment, sport and recreational expenses, cars, cycles, and vans, fashionable clothes, drugs, and alcohol. School, for many youth, is not primarily for education.

All this is not to say that contemporary youth are worse than previous generations. It's to say that times have changed, and possibly one of the most unfortunate turns has been the development of the teen subculture (which the teens did not develop). Building on youth's vulnerability, the creators of teen music and fashions have constructed a world built upon the pleasure principle: gratification NOW, as much and as often as possible. If it feels good, do it!

Especially vulnerable are the young teens, junior high age. It is this age group that is often effectively lured away from family and church, and from the wholesome influences they desperately need but frequently have been encouraged to avoid.

Families, churches, and schools must not relinquish their responsibilities toward the young at this critical time, while they are in junior and senior high school. In most cases, parents are the best thing that kids have going for themselves. Then why, it must be asked, do so many parents give up the raising of their teens to popular song-writers, television producers, and youth's peers? Who is raising the children?

1. Parents and teachers are encouraged to explore honestly with young people their patterns of socializing, whether in large or small groups, pairing, going with, going steady, or whatever. Young people will almost always have their own terminology and their own set of standards and criteria for their dating relationships. Adults will not be communicating accurately with them unless they come to terms with the meanings of words and the significance of the experience. It will be essential to define the terms.

To some, the term *dating* will designate a fairly exclusive relationship, to others it will designate a much more tentative one. Many young people do not consider themselves in a dating relationship even though they may have paired off with one other person. A phrase they use is "going with." This is not the same as "going steady." To them, "going with" signifies a degree of exclusiveness in a relationship, in some way, "I am yours, you are mine." There may or may not be a sign of this exclusiveness, such as, an exchange of rings or some other possession. Going steady will probably mean a relationship that is exclusive, interdependent, mutually determined, and intended to continue for the foreseeable future. Going steady precedes engagement and is more serious than "going with."

2. For younger adolescents, group experiences are recommended over pairing.

Youth is the time to open out, not narrow in. Young people need the wise and prudent guidance their parents and teachers can give. Without this guidance, many young people jump into adult-type experiences of dating before they are ready and while they are very vulnerable. Before a young person goes on his or her first date, much preparation should have taken place. Many youth feel that dating is no business of their parents or adults; hence, they neither will ask them nor anyone else, nor will they accept in a receptive spirit the advice and counsel offered by adults. Parents and other caring adults do have a responsibility for the development of young people during adolescence. Junior high youth are not ready for dating.

Sometime during senior high, most youth will be ready for dating. They should always be encouraged to double date or triple date, that is, plan their time of recreation and socializing with one or two other couples. This kind of experience is a natural transition from the grouping experiences of earlier adolescence. Young people will understand the natural gradation if it is pointed out to them. When two persons date, what maturity is required of them? When are they ready for dating? What do they need to know prior to their first dating experience? What responsibilities should they be capable of, and what strengths should they have? What should they know in order to benefit positively from dating?

3. Awareness of the purposes of dating can bring greater benefits from the experience.

Among the commonly recognized purposes are:

a. Learning to relate in positive and acceptable ways with others.

b. Developing capacities and abilities in social, athletic, and recreational activities.

c. Discovering self through interaction with other people of one's age group.

d. Becoming acquainted with other persons one's own age.

e. Growing in the ability to respect and reverence other persons.

f. Ultimately to find the one person to share life within marriage.

Awareness of these purposes can help young people avoid certain dangers and mistakes. Association with friends and peers should result in (a) deepening mutual reverence, (b) deepening self-discipline, and (c) increased ability to value more worthwhile things. It is important that young people know that "something genuinely good" must come from their relationships. If not, something may be wrong.

4. Adolescents are developing into adults, learning to be independent, responsible, wholesome, and self-confident.

Dating experiences can help a person to develop in many areas, including the development of one's talents. Sharing an interest with another person is a great motivation for self-development. Dating helps young people to clarify and reinforce their values. What do they believe, and how strongly do they believe certain ideas? Ultimately, of course, adolescents who date prepare themselves for marriage and, as a matter of fact, for single adulthood as well.

5. Before adolescents date, they should have developed a set of standards or criteria which they will use to guide their dating experiences.

The following are suggested as criteria:

Date someone you like and who is trustworthy.

Set limits to signs of affection.

Determine how frequently you ought to date and the types of activity.

Establish reasonable criteria for using the car.
Decide never to use drugs or drink on a date.

Young people need to be encouraged very much by parents and teachers so that they will know it is acceptable to establish criteria and to set limits to their dating activities. They need the support that parents and teachers can give.

6. Some youth begin to date without any awareness of the dangers and the pitfalls they might encounter.
Thinking that they are quite adult, they wander off into areas that are dangerous to their lives as well as to their morals. One counselor who has been working in a clinic for several years remarked that every year, approximately six weeks after the drive-in movies open in the spring, a rush of pregnant girls would appear at the threshold. In an earlier day, drive-in movies were sometimes referred to as "passion pits." Evidently this has not changed. Should not young people be forewarned and therefore forearmed? What are some of the dangers about which parents and teachers should counsel teenagers?

Besides pointing out the dangers, of course, parents and teachers can encourage positive habits. Teenagers should feel welcome to bring their friends, companions, and dates home. They need to learn how to make introductions and how to incorporate their friends into family and home. Parents can encourage children to bring their friends home and to share their friends in family gatherings.

7. Not much has been said in recent years about appropriateness of dress.
Almost all cultural limits in regard to dress have been challenged and broken. Society seems to have gone from "cover-all" to the "nude-look." Dress does make a difference. How people dress does express something about their personalities. The exterior does manifest something about the interior. Dress on either men or women which accents the genitals suggests a

genital view of sexuality. It is difficult to deny that a genital accent promotes exploitative relationships. Young people need to be encouraged to be careful and prudent about their dress, as they work to develop an integrated and wholesome personal sexuality.

8. Alcohol is one of the most commonly used and most abused chemicals.

The high incidence of drinking to excess among youth is alarming. There seems to be an almost cavalier attitude about drink. The dangers to safety, sexual integrity, and future are overlooked and neglected. Parents and teachers should explore with young people their attitudes toward alcoholic consumption, the civil laws concerning alcoholic use by minors, alcoholic consumption among adults, and the destruction of lives brought about by alcohol. Youth should be encouraged to follow the simple rule of never drinking on a date.

9. One of the fastest ways to totally "mess up" a life is through the use of drugs.

As with drink, drugs are a form of abuse of one's body and comprise a serious danger to health. Youth should be advised never to take drugs on a date, or at any time for that matter. Drugs are most often used as an escape from reality to unreality. As such they do not help people cope with the real world. Young people need to learn that it is much better to face difficulties and challenges and even boredom than to escape or attempt to escape through chemical experimentation or use.

Abuse of chemicals, whether alcohol or drugs, weakens self-control and diminishes self-direction. One of the real tragedies of chemical abuse is the loss of control over one's life, whether that loss be partial or complete.

LESSON 8   LIST OF TERMS

Dating
Social engagement between a male and female person.

Exclusiveness
Quality of a relationship between certain persons that shuts out all others.

"Going With"
Used in some circles to mean a degree of exclusiveness in a relationship, but not as limited as *going steady*.

Group Experiences
Several persons enjoying themselves in common socializing events.

Honesty
The quality of being free from deception; genuine; real; sincere; truthful.

Independence
Controlling oneself; freedom from another's control; having self-determination.

Interactions
Mutual action or influence; relationships between persons.

Socialization
Process of learning to relate with other persons in ways that are socially acceptable.

Standard
Rule or criterion used to guide behavior.

Value
Something of worth, utility, or importance. Moral value is a moral good, e.g., honesty, respect, faithfulness.

9 Serious Consequences of Sexual Activity

Marla was one of those simple, slightly naive kids who believed it couldn't happen the first time. But it did. Pregnant at sixteen, she replayed the episode over and over again in her mind, each with a different ending. Those were the dreams, the fantasies. The reality was that she was six months pregnant and resigned to give up the baby for adoption. The decision hadn't been easy—to go against the trend. She took some strength in knowing that she had already bucked the trend in choosing not to abort.

The night she became pregnant, her boyfriend Russ had had quite a bit to drink. She never saw him so affectionate and aggressive. Some of his comments had made her feel sexually stupid, a feeling she neither liked nor completely understood, so she acquiesced and followed his lead.

Later, when they confirmed the pregnancy, Russ felt remorse. He realized that he had taken advantage of Marla and forced himself upon her. He couldn't shake the guilt. He had tried to make up for his behavior by staying closer now, visiting or calling her everyday. Marla's feelings towards him were becoming more and more confused. At times she didn't know if she felt love or hate. She couldn't wait until the whole thing was over, whenever that would be. Could it be never?

Sexual activity among American teenagers has become a national concern. The high rate of pregnancies and the epidemic of venereal disease are pressuring adults to take a more serious look at adolescent sexual patterns. Caught in their own web of experiences, hang-ups, convictions, values, confusions, and bewilderment, many adults simply throw up their hands and surrender in a posture of silence. Since no one wants to be "sexually ignorant," it is often easier and less risky to avoid confronting self, spouse, or teen on the subject. As a result, the trends continue.

Although statistics are not available from earlier times that could prove a significant increase in sexual activity among today's teens compared with their parent's or grandparent's generation, the feeling is common that it is so. Discussion of this issue can be a way of avoiding the problem before us. However, the real question is: What are our youth doing, and is it wholesome and moral; if not, what should we, their parents and teachers, be doing about it?

The facts these days are that close to half the nation's high schoolers engage in premarital sex, and that their initial experiences are happening at an earlier age. More pregnancies are occuring among junior high school youth, and venereal disease is now rampant among adolescents, accounting for a significant number among all reported cases.

In a sense, the kids are caught between divergent and conflicting philosophies, developing theologies, and changing societal standards. The value of abstinence is being displaced by pleasureable indulgence. The Church even recognizes more openly the rightful place of pleasure. Furthermore, in our culture sexual involvement no longer sparks the disapproval it used to. Obviously, parents and the adult generation also feel caught in the same conflicts. How long before we recover our balance enough to renew our convictions about sexual morals and standards and reveal them to the young we love and want so much to teach?

1. In spite of the times, parents still have the primary influence on their child's sexual and moral values.

Parents who give witness to fidelity, tenderness, responsible relationships, value toward life, and chastity are already handing on a powerful message which is forming and shaping the value system of the child. Can they say more? Yes, much more, especially in guiding the young regarding sexual activity. Certainly parents have, not only the right, but the responsibility to guide their children in all moral matters. Those who suggest that teens are old enough to make decisions about sex without the guidance of their parents make a serious mistake.

As teens get older, certainly more and more of their decision-making will necessarily be more independent and private, as they mature and internalize values as well as become more totally responsible for their own lives. Parents are more responsible for the choices younger adolescents make, and they are held to be so responsible in other areas, such as, teenage driving, drinking, treatment of property, and similar types of activities. Yet, in regard to sex, parents face a real dilemma: They are told, on the one hand, that their child's sex activity is a private matter, and on the other, that their child's pregnancy is their (the parent's) responsibility. Sex is a moral matter with serious social consequences, and without question falls within the guiding arena for parents.

This chapter considers two very serious consequences of teenage sexual activity: pregnancy and venereal disease. They are considered together because of their seriousness and prevalence, and because both demand a more definite and effective response from parents, teachers, and adults generally. Pregnancy is not a disease, as syphilis and gonorrhea are, but its impact upon our youth today is as frightening and disruptive as VD or any other serious youth problem.

Any society which loves its children and youth will commit its resources to finding better ways to assist them in their growth even if this means sharing "do's and don'ts," confronting their desires and wants, challenging their values, and urging them toward responsible adulthood. Parents, teachers, clergy, and others may find it necessary to do some hard work and preparation if they are to meet the moral needs of the present generation of youth.

2. This year again, more than one million pregnancies are likely to occur among teenage girls.

The pattern in recent years has been that sixty percent of these pregnancies will come to term, and forty percent will be aborted. Of those who are born, more than ninety percent will be kept by the mother who will try to raise him or her as a single parent. Some will marry in order "to give the child a name" but the rate of failure in such marriages is very high.

Less than ten percent give up their babies for adoption. Little more than a decade ago, the numbers giving up their child for adoption and the numbers keeping their child were reversed.

Statistics indicate a high incidence of battered children with teenage mothers. Most teens do not have the maturity to cope with the needs of a child over a long period of time, and too often the result is uncontrollable anger and violence. There is also a high suicide rate among teenage mothers, and unmarried mothers often experience a great deal of isolation. Their friends usually come around the first few months after the birth but rather quickly tire of the limitations which their friend is under. Pregnancy is currently the greatest cause for the high school drop-out rate. Many young mothers quit school and as a result never complete their education. Unmarried teenage mothers often experience unbearable financial hardships, and many develop a dependency on welfare which continues into adulthood.

In a very real sense, pregnancy for a very young teen can be dangerous to health. The death risk for young pregnant girls is sixty percent higher due to hemorrhage and toxemia. They are also more likely than older mothers to catch diseases, because the pregnancy depletes the nutrition their own body needs for adolescent growth.

78

3. The rights of the male parent of the child are largely ignored.
The laws give practically no recourse or rights to the father.
If the mother wishes to have an abortion and the father does
not, the mother's will prevails.

A study of sex and the teenage boy suggests that many young
males' attitudes towards sexuality are very immature. Often
young men are almost cavalier in their attitudes, treating the
girl simply as a sex object. For many of them contraception is
the woman's responsibility, and whatever happens as a result
of intercourse happens "in her body, not mine."

For a long period of time there has been a double standard
for males and females relative to sexual activity. For some
reason it is supposedly okay for a man to "sow his wild oats"
but not okay for a woman. Similarily, the married man's affair
is not judged as bad as the married woman's affair. Much effort
needs to be expended in order to change present attitudes of
men toward women as sexual objects.

4. What happens to the child of teenage parents?
Babies of young teens are two to three times more likely to die
in their first year compared with babies of mothers who are in
their early twenties. They are more likely to be born with
emotional and neurological defects. Most of these babies live
their beginning years without a father to parent them, and
babies born to teenagers are a lot more likely to be premature
and weigh less.

The Papal Committee for the Family has published a report
entitled "The Family in the Pastoral Activity of the Church."
In this document the Committee states that a child has a natural right to have a father and a mother. It is easy to develop
from this statement the natural right of the child to be born
into a cradle of commitment, that is, a union of mother and
father which is sealed by marriage. A person does not have to
reflect for very long on nature and its requirements for the
healthy upbringing of children. There can be little doubt that

God designed marriage and the family and put them at the very basis of our society.

More and more studies are being done which look at the phenomenon of teenage pregnancy and parenting. These studies bring out some startling facts. For example, many girls who become pregnant want to; some because of their need for love, others because a baby happens to be a status symbol in their environment. There is a curious romanticism evident in much of the phenomenon.

Others see abortion as the quick and easy way out, a fast solution to a difficult pregnancy. The long-range problems of abortion are not dealt with adequately, for example, the guilt that lingers, and the possible physical damage to the young mother. For some mothers, abortions damage their health in ways that make the later bearing of children more difficult, if not impossible.

It should be deeply impressed upon teenagers that parenting requires responsibility. Teenagers who have children are not ready to be parents. Being a parent is challenging enough even within a stable marriage. It is very difficult outside of marriage.

5. Gonorrhea is the most common serious infectious disease in the United States today.

Gonorrhea, commonly called "the clap" or "the drip," seldom causes death but it can cause sterility and crippling arthritis if it is not treated immediately. It can also result in blindness and heart disease. The symptoms of gonorrhea are usually quite evident in a man, because within a few days after infection he will notice a painful sensation when he urinates and pus will drop from his penis. In a woman, the symptoms are not easily noticeable since the germs usually live and multiply within her body around the cervix. Anyone suspecting gonorrhea should submit to a medical examination immediately so that treatment can begin. The treatment is simple—usually a few shots of penicillin. Though this will usually cure a person it will not give immunity. If left untreated the germs spread throughout the body damaging the sex organs and bone joints.

Gonorrhea is epidemic throughout the world today. There are some new strains of the disease showing up that cannot be stopped with any available antibiotic. It appears that penicillin is losing some of its effectiveness as new strains of the gonorrhea germ show great resistance to available cures. Herpes II is a type of venereal disease which is incurable. This virus causes several diseases including shingles, chicken pox, and mononucleosis. Unlike Herpes I which produces cold sores on the mouth or face, Herpes II usually causes blisterlike sores on or near the genitals, often accompanied by fever, swollen lymph glands, and muscle aches.

Thousands annually go blind as a result of the disease. Female herpes victims are more likely to develop cervical cancer, and pregnant women with an active infection pass on the disease to their babies in one out of two cases. Many of these babies will suffer brain damage or blindness. Some will die because of it. Scientists are struggling to find a cure.

6. Syphilis is the third most infectious disease common in the United States.
It can result in blindness, heart disease, insanity, paralysis, and even death. If a woman with the disease becomes pregnant, her baby may be stillborn, or blind, or otherwise defective. Syphilis can remain undetected for years since the germs tend to go "underground" after the symptoms disappear. They remain latent for long periods of time before breaking out into another siege. While undetected, the germs may spread throughout the body damaging organs and causing serious health problems. Usually syphilis is transmitted by sexual intercourse, however it can also be spread by "deep kissing" with the person who has a canker sore in his or her mouth. Both gonorrhea and syphilis can be passed on to another person during heavy petting. Syphilis is cured with large dosages of penicillin or other

antibiotics. As with gonorrhea, special tests given by a doctor can detect the presence of the disease.

Young people should be made aware of the facts about venereal disease. They should realize the seriousness of the health dangers involved, the difficulty in detecting the disease, especially in women, because of the lack of evident symptoms, and the fact that new viruses are present today which defy cure.

7. Many infected persons or even those who suspect venereal disease fear medical attention because they do not want to risk becoming known.

Not confident that their medical personnel will keep confidentiality, they delay and even put off totally the detection kinds of services they require. Young people should be helped to realize that even worse than having the disease itself is not getting it treated. Clinics are available and teen medical centers do provide confidential medical treatment for young people. Pamphlets and other means of information are available from the State Department of Public Health.

8. Adults can help youth see that many of the reasons they have for having sexual intercourse and for conceiving a child are not good reasons.

The male who wants "a boy," usually to name after himself, may be deluded with poor self-image or a false sense of manliness. Is he ready, able, and committed to provide a home, and education, and the love and faithful presence necessary to raise a child? The female who wants someone she can love unconditionally and who will respond dependently to her love may still be caught up in the turmoil of adolescent growth, struggling with self-worth and identity. Is she ready, able and committed to be a full-time parent? (Is there such a thing as a "part-time" parent?)

9. Christian parents have, in their religious tradition, strong support for giving their children guidance in sexual matters, and for sharing with them their appreciation of parenting and the grave responsibility it entails.

Teens who engage in premarital sexual intercourse need to know that they are violating Christian moral norms. Enough reasons can be given to back up these Christian teachings. What is so often lacking, it would appear, is courage—enough to enable parents and teachers to get what they want to share with youth out of their hearts and into their vocal cords. Besides Christian witness and good example, youth need to be told in words. In a day and age when everybody else is telling them what to do about sex, why not their own parents?

Gonorrhea
Type of venereal disease; a contagious inflammation of the genital mucous membrane caused by the germ *conococcus*.

Moral Norm
Principle of right action.

Pregnancy Testing
Examination to prove whether or not a woman is pregnant, and includes urine specimen and pelvic examination.

Prenatal Care
Watchful attention, medical and emotional, during pregnancy to protect and nurture the well-being of both the mother and her developing baby.

Single Parent
Only one parent, either a mother or a father, rearing one or more children without the regular assistance of the other parent due to separation, divorce, or death.

Sterilization
Procedure of making one incapable of having children; also an outcome resulting from VD in some victims.

Syphilis
Chronic, contagious venereal, and often congenital, disease caused by the germ *spirochete*; a type of venereal disease, similar to gonorrhea.

Teenage Parenting
Parents still in their teens responsible for the rearing and education of their child.

Venereal Disease (VD)
Contagious disease that is typically transmitted by sexual intercourse.

Genital Herpes
Viral venereal disease. Consequences are serious and no effective remedy has been found.

10 The Choice for Chastity

Lord knows it was hard enough raising kids with two parents; now she was doing the job alone, except for two weekends a month when their father had them. Jacinta prayed every night before falling off to sleep that the two boys, aged 15 and 17, would not get any girls "into trouble." Grandma kept telling her that girls were harder to raise, but Jacinta did not find it so. It was the boys she worried about. They never told her anything, even when she asked and begged them to communicate.

Her girls, the oldest and the youngest of the four, communicated all the time, something a mother could be grateful for. Carla, aged 19, had always been serious as a child and exceptionally responsible. Never a flirt, she had the highest moral standards and the backbone to live by them. So far it had been easy to guide her in her dating experiences, since the trust between them was deep and strong. Both treasured their relationship. As for Lupe, the youngest, time would tell. Jacinta was sure that Lupe was scarred as a child, probably permanently, by her father's obscene behavior twice when he was drunk.

What haunted Jacinta most was her fear that the boys were taking after their father. She had seen them, in separate incidents, become quite physically involved with a neighbor girl. She knew that they hung around the "dirty magazine" rack at the drugstore and that their language more frequently of late displayed a cavalier attitude towards women. She had tried to get them involved with Denny, the parish youth minister whose manliness didn't need to be bolstered by cheap treatment of women. How does a mother teach her sons to respect their own sexuality and to have a proper regard for the other sex? She wished she had a better handle on it.

Within any given group of adolescents there will be great variations in maturity. Some appear quite mature and ready to discuss almost any topic a parent or teacher raises. Others seem to be living in another world—most likely the world of the child—and they will not relate as quickly nor as consciously to the discussion. The teacher and parent have to realize that great differences do exist among teens, that there are young people at both ends of the spectrum, in order to tend sensitively to their needs.

The teacher or parent should have some confidence in the youngster, even though the communication and feedback from the teenager may appear to be negligible. Oftentimes teens simply do not let others know what they are thinking, but they are thinking. More than one teacher of adolescents has remarked at the end of a class that the students appeared uninterested. Hours later the teacher discovered that the students heard every word and, indeed, were even quoting the teacher.

A good rule to follow in moral education is to teach by the norm, not by the exception. Teach the general principles, the moral maxims. Do not begin with examples which detail a set of circumstances justifying exceptions to the rule. Teenagers' intellectual powers of abstraction are not well-developed enough to handle this. The younger the child the more necessary it is to spell out the general norms with specific rules. Too often adults fail to realize that youth simply do not have the experience, maturity, or intellectual development to act morally with only the most general of norms to guide them.

After all, those who encourage youth to get sexually involved are giving them more than abstract ideas. Turn on the radio and listen to the songs that the youngsters listen to. Parents who do this are shocked and amazed at the explicitness and directness of some of the lyrics. Many popular love songs which are listened to again and again, daily, by the youngsters, promote sexual expression and intercourse as a common and expected thing. Christian youth need a great deal of support and encouragement today to live out the teaching of Jesus and the moral norms expressed by the Church. Many of them want to live a chaste Christian life. They need and deserve our expressions of encouragement and support.

1. Chastity is that part of the virtue of temperance which regulates the use of the power of sex.
Chastity is not limited to simply avoiding the faults and sins against sexuality. It is aimed at attaining higher and positive goals. Chastity concerns itself with the entire personality, both interior and exterior. It not only guides what one does sexually but also what one desires sexually.

Chastity is part of the virtue of temperance. Temperance aims at self-preservation, by controlling the instinct for the conservation of the bodily life of the individual (food and drink) and also by controlling the desire for the conservation of the human species (sex instinct). Both categories of instincts, that is, of bodily life and human species, must be subordinated as means to their end and purpose. They become forces of destruction if they are made ends rather than means. Temperance subordinates them to the pattern intended by God. Temperance admits God as the supreme and most lovable good. All other goods must be placed in relation to God. Temperance aims at the proper order. If a person were to love himself or herself more than God, he or she would love in a disordered manner. The instincts of self-preservation and preservation of the race can become disordered and rebellious. The role of temperance is to balance and control, through the dual means of self-understanding and self-discipline.

2. There are three types of chastity.

Consecrated virginity is one type of chastity for those who are called and who accept the total dedication of their lives to God and to the service of His people. Secondly, there is the chastity for those who are married. Thirdly, there is the chastity for the unmarried single person, whether that person be single by choice or circumstance or simply too young to be married. We will discuss each.

Some Christians are called to publicly dedicate their lives to God. They bind themselves to total dedication through the vow of chastity or some other sacred bond which has a similar purpose. "By such a bond, a person is totally dedicated to God, loved above all things. In this way, that person is ordained to the honor and service of God under a new and special title." Vowed chastity is one of the evangelical counsels. The counsels are special gifts of God to the Church. They foster the holiness of the Church in a special way. "An eminent position among these is held by virginity or the celibate state. This is a precious gift of divine grace given by God to certain souls, whereby they may devote themselves to God alone the more easily, due to an undivided heart" (Constitution on the Church, no. 42). Vowed chastity or celibacy places a person totally in the service of love of God and neighbor.

Within marriage the virtue of chastity guides the interaction of husband and wife in their married love. It brings the measure of self-restraint, self-control, and reverence that married love needs if it is to deepen in true charity. Husband and wife are called to hold each other in respect. Their love is vowed in the exchange of promises given on the day of their wedding. Married persons must remain chaste and develop the virtue of chastity. In every marriage there are certain times when the sexual expression of intercourse is impossible, requiring self-restraint. When business, work, or a career separate husband and wife for a time, chastity will preserve their faithfulness to each other. When a woman is pregnant and finds sexual intercourse undesirable or impossible, chaste love will deepen their faithfulness. In their family planning, husband and wife learn that restraint consciously and willingly endured can be a source of growth in their love and faithfulness.

There is a third type of chastity, this one for those neither vowed to be celibate nor vowed in a marriage bond. This type is for those who are called to live out their baptismal promises as single persons or who for one reason or another have not yet found a marriage partner. This type includes those who are widowed or separated. It even includes those for whom celibacy has been "imposed," that is, because of psychological or physical handicaps they must live a celibate life. The moral norms guiding unmarried persons are the two norms stated next.

3. There are two moral norms which guide the use of sex previous to marriage.
The first is that sexual intercourse belongs only in marriage. The second norm follows from this; sexual activity which prepares for intercourse also belongs only in marriage. These two norms should be taught simply and clearly. Discussion about them is essential as well as learning to apply them to life. In an earlier day it was enough for parents or teachers to give the moral norm and say that was enough. For many, that *was* enough. Today's youngsters, perhaps because of the type of education they are receiving, require more than the norm. They ask for and have a right to hear the reasons behind the norms. There are many reasons in Christian tradition why a couple should "wait until marriage" before engaging in foreplay and sexual intercourse. For one, bearing children outside of marriage is gravely irresponsible, considering the permanent and serious consequences to the child, mother, father, and others. For another, fornication violates God's law. Some teens may not be ready to understand why God forbids premarital sex, while for others, the following ideas may be helpful.

Teens who become sexually active risk "premature bonding," that is, being sexually involved before their individual identities are established. In "premature bonding" two personalities merge and bond together. Like two young trees growing too close to each other, neither gets the sunlight and nourishment they would receive were they planted farther apart, and neither one grows truly strong, free, and independent. Premature lovers also isolate themselves from family and friends and often cut themselves away from opportunities they need to develop full personalities. Premarital sex sets them up for hurt, morally, emotionally, and psychologically, and it can cause harm to a future marriage if guilt lingers on because of failure in self-restraint prior to marriage.

A prevalent attitude today is the contraceptive mentality. Many adults promote the use of contraceptives among unmarried young people assuming that they are going to be sexually active. They give youth no credit for being virtuous nor do they even set such an expectation. This attitude sells youth short. They are capable of self-restraint and moral virtue. The Church believes they can and will live positive lives of chastity if encouraged.

4. Young people today need the encouragement and the example of others if they are to choose the way of chastity over the pleasure principle of contemporary culture.

It is not that Christians deny the pleasure of sex and reject its joy. Not at all. Rather, sexual pleasure is cherished as a gift from God, but a gift that requires, as do all God's gifts, a respect for the purpose which God ordained and the boundaries which He established.

Respect for purpose and boundaries is the starting point for growth in chastity. Young people require some assistance in defining and developing a chaste love. Especially helpful is some discussion of the quality of tenderness and affection as an expression of love. Tenderness is a motor expression, that is, a movement of the person towards another. It involves an expression of the heart through the eyes or through words of tenderness, or through touch.

How does a person grow in tenderness? First, the relationship must be rooted in genuine love. One must be honestly concerned and desirous for the welfare of the other. Secondly, the expression of this love in sight, sound, and touch must be an act of genuine love. A person learns tenderness as he or she learns anything else, through experience, reflection on the experience, and a constant desire to grow in love.

A particular sign can mean very different things, given different people and situations. For example, a kiss between a brother and sister is a very different experience than a kiss between lovers. The chaste embrace of a mother and a child is very different from an embrace between lovers or sexual partners. Youngsters who have witnessed the chaste love of their parents have learned the basic lessons of tenderness, appropriate signs of affection, and chaste love. Youth should be encouraged to learn early the difference between a sign of affection which signifies genuine care and a sign of affection which signifies sexual desire and want. Knowing this distinction will help them assess their relationships and give direction to their lives.

It is not that kissing is good and sexual desire is bad. After all, God created the affections and passions and gave them a purpose. Each person must learn to become responsible in using them. Knowing oneself is an essential step in achieving this.

5. Genuine affection and care for another person is often expressed through the sense of touch.
Light kissing, hand-holding, sitting close, placing one's arm around another's waist or shoulders are all appropriate and legitimate expressions of affection and love. Many today call this "necking." Of course, to be legitimate, signs of affection cannot be forced upon another person, but rather must be received and accepted as well as offered and given. These kinds

of touch are not meant to arouse a person to sexual intercourse and they are not expressions of sexual desire as such. Measured against the moral norms given earlier and defined as above, necking can be an appropriate affectionate expression for the unmarried.

Other kinds of touch, for example, caressing and deep kissing, are meant to arouse sexual desire and prepare for intercourse. These are appropriate for a married couple as they are preparing for intercourse. Many use the term "petting" to describe these kinds of touch.

Another fact that young people should know is the difference between a boy's and a girl's response in a love relationship. The initial as well as dominant experience for the boy tends to be physical. The initial and dominant experience for the girl tends to be emotional. For the boy, it centers in the physical sexual desire, while for the girl it centers in the desire for union of hearts. The girl should know that boys tend to be aroused physically very quickly and very strongly. Boys should know that girls tend to feel commitment of their hearts. There may be more truth than one would like to admit in the observation of a TV reporter concluding a story about teens and sex: boys play at love in order to get sex while girls play at sex in order to get love.

6. Youth can understand growth in relationships better if they see the natural steps in its development.
This model is suggested.

    a. From acquaintance to a new friend.
    b. From a new friend to a trusted and loyal friend.
    c. From a trusted and loyal friend to a steady companion.
    d. From a steady companion to an engaged relationship with intent to marry.
    e. From engagement to a marriage commitment.

Using this model and discussing the kinds of affection, the most appropriate at the various stages, and including in the discussion the two moral norms given above, youth can learn to work out for themselves appropriate forms of expression. It might also be helpful for them to know that the closer to marriage they get in a relationship the more likely it is that greater restraint, not less, will be demanded.

In discussions with young people about affectionate expressions, it is important to affirm the wholesomeness of affectionate activities that are genuine, personal, and appropriate. The Church does not condemn affectionate expressions but rather encourages them.

A word should be said at this point about sexual arousal which is involuntary. In both males and females sexual feelings and responses can occur unintentionally. This can happen while expressing appropriate affection, by just being close together, or sharing personal thoughts in conversation. Such sexual arousal is not wrong and will usually subside by a change of topic or position or by focusing one's attention on the relationship, rather than on the sexual feelings.

7. What young people experience in their own families is of utmost importance in their development of chastity.
Vatican Council II in the Church in the Modern World, no. 49, states:

> . . . It is imperative to give suitable and timely instruction to young people, above all in the heart of their own families, about the dignity of married love, its role and its exercise; in this way they will be able to engage in honorable courtship and enter upon marriage of their own.

Instruction in the family usually will be informal with mother and/or dad choosing a time to discuss the facts of life and the content of sex education. The purpose of such education is to lead youth to grow in chastity. (The Church is committed to assist the family in instruction of their youth.)

Another aid in the development of chastity is the young person's relationship to Christ. Both prayer and the sacraments can help the young person to develop a personal relationship to the Lord and Savior. After all, it is Jesus who shows us the way to peace and happiness. It is Jesus who calls us away from selfishness and lust to unselfishness and chaste love.

One of the special means that God gives people to help them in the development of chastity (as well as other virtues) is counsel, the seeking and receiving of advice and wisdom from others. Surely every person has need of counsel at certain times in life. Especially when important decisions are being considered and when crises are being anticipated or actually experienced is counsel appropriate and necessary. Many people find great difficulty being objective in matters of sexuality. Since pleasure has a way of "blinding" a person to facts, the possibility of self-deception is great. All the more reason to take advantage of the maturity and judgment of one who has passed through a particular experience successfully.

8. In this chapter our concentration has been on chastity for unmarried persons.

The three main sins against chastity for the unmarried are masturbation, premarital sex, and homosexual activity. Masturbation is sinful because of its selfish orientation and because it is against the norms of marriage. Premarital sex and premarital intercourse are sinful because they are intimacies which belong within the commitment of marriage. Homosexual activities are sinful because they violate the procreative purpose of sex.

Sin is a deliberate offense against the laws of God. It is a deliberate turning away from the moral norms given us by God. Sexual sins are best understood in relation to all sin. Sometimes immorality is equated with sexual sins whereas, in fact, sex is only one part of the moral life. It is important to see sexual morality in perspective with morality in other areas, such as honesty, and respect for property and persons.

9. Rape and incest are two serious crimes involving sex which need informed understanding and professional treatment.
Rape is the fastest growing crime in some communities. It is considered more an act of violence than of sexual passion since evidence indicates that the assailant uses sex in order to conquer another or act out aggressive feelings. Many communities provide informational programs and speakers giving helpful insights on the prevention, reporting, and treatment of rape.

Contrary to popular feelings, most rape victims "do not ask for it." The majority of rapes are at least partially preplanned. Victims are of every age, race, social class, and shape. Rapists attack as often in private residences as not. Sometimes rapist and victims are acquaintances, and even related. In most cases, the woman is physically threatened and harmed. The vast majority of rapes involve a rapist and victim of the same race and economic class. Rapists are not "sex fiends," but tend to have normal sex drives with a stronger than average tendency to be violent and aggressive.

Unfortunately, few rapists are apprehended and convicted for their crimes. The high incidence of rape calls for concerted efforts on the part of local communities to develop effective deterrents and procedures to prevent and treat this particular violent crime.

Incest has been called the "silent crime." Defined as the sexual abuse of a minor by a parent, guardian, or caretaker, incest is psychologically damaging to the victim and to other family members. Low self-esteem, depression, guilt, confusion, and ambivalence concerning sexuality are usual emotional consequences. Offenders need serious counselling as well as the victims. However, the responsibility of the state is first to the victim.

A child often has no one else to protect himself or herself from abusive parents or legal guardians. The rights of parents over their children and the rights of adults to privacy add to the sensitivity of treating incest situations. Mandatory reporting laws are becoming more common and are helping to protect children from family sexual abuse. Since evidence suggests that incest patterns are transferred from generation to generation, that is, abused children tend to become abusive adults, intervention of some kind is probably necessary if the pattern is to be broken.

Various forms of guilt are often present in offenders and victims of both rape and incest. Compassion must be accompanied by wise counsel if healing and positive growth are to result from these most difficult and very painful experiences.

LESSON 10   LIST OF TERMS

Adultery

Sexual intercourse by a married person with a person other than spouse.

Chastity

Form of temperance which regulates sexual desire and activity according to God's design. The capacity to use and enjoy sex according to Christian moral norms.

Contraceptive Mentality

Attitude that since contraceptives are readily available they are the best means to prevent pregnancy; abstinence is either not considered at all or is thought to be "old-fashioned."

Making Out

This term can refer to either necking or petting.

Necking

Usually understood to include light kissing, hand-holding, sitting close, or placing one's arm around another's waist or shoulders.

Petting

Usually understood to include deep kissing, caressing the most sensitive parts of the body; involves the kind of touching that prepares a couple for sexual intercourse.

Premarital Intercourse

Sexual union of a male and female person before marriage.

Premarital Sex

Mutual sex play; the term may include intercourse.

"Premature Bonding"

A very intimate and early involvement which interferes with or delays individual maturation. Personalities of boy and girl are too close for each to develop freely as individuals.

Virginity

Refraining from sexual intercourse while unmarried. This term applies to both men and women.

11 Responsibility for Unitive and Procreative Purposes

When Nancy and Tom were married twenty-five years ago, they expected to begin their family right away. Nancy laughs now whenever she recalls her disappointment two months after their wedding. Here she was, married two months and not pregnant yet. Was she sterile? Would she never bear a child?

Seven children and a silver anniversary later, they clearly see the contrast between their first year of marriage and their recently-married daughter's. Times have changed, they observe with mixed feelings. Today's newlyweds seem to have a different order of priorities, with children being important certainly, but "not yet" and "not many."

To Tom and Nancy, their daughter and son-in-law seem to be much more thoughtful and deliberate about raising a family than they had been. In the late '50s young couples anticipated having large families. They believed it was a blessing and that somehow God would provide.

Had they been presumptuous or naive? Was their children's generation smarter? These are difficult questions. Yes, it was a challenge to rear and educate seven children, and more than once their limits were tested. Yet, they loved their children, each of them, including the two "rhythm babies" and one "complete surprise."

Nancy and Tom were trying to get used to the idea that it might be three or four years before they would be grandparents. The whole notion of family planning seemed

*to them to deny some of the spontaneity and a bit of the
mystery which had surrounded their own child-bearing
experiences. They hoped that the younger generation would
leave room in their planning "for God's surprises."*

*Well, they mused, they can't lead their grown children's
lives. Perhaps they themselves would do it differently were
they just starting out. On second thought, perhaps not. Life
would be so diminished for them without Barbara, David,
Robert, Jessica, Trina, Billy, and Sarah.*

Many junior and senior high school sex education programs
present detailed information on birth control and the variety
of methods available today. Such an approach and emphasis
does not respect the basic value and belief systems of the vast
majority who disapprove of teens being sexually active. For
youth's sake adults do more if they assume youth are not going
to be sexually active, rather than assuming the alternative.
Youth who are engaging in sexual intercourse need to be challenged first with reasons why they would be well advised to
"wait until marriage." The presumption, wrongly, is that they
have a right to be sexually active.

From every Christian perspective conceivable, sex is not ex-
empt from God's laws and purpose. Rather than concentrating
on methods of birth control, sex education programs should
emphasize the purpose of marriage and sex within marriage.
The problems of teen pregnancies and parenthood, abortion,
school dropouts, and the host of other complications will not
be resolved without parents taking stronger leadership in their
sons' and daughters' moral education.

Whether actual or not, discussions in the 1960s about morality in marriage always seemed to center on moral and immoral methods of birth control. By the time Paul VI published
Humanae Vitae restating the Church's traditional ban on artificial means, many Catholic couples had decided their own

conscience in the matter, some leaving the Church over this issue, others staying in officially but choosing to ignore this particular Church teaching, and still others unsure of what they should do.

The question remains a sensitive and difficult one for many Catholics. However, today's discussion seems focused less on means of birth control and more on the conciliar doctrine about the coessential purposes of marriage. Today when birth control is discussed, many couples are ready to recognize the dangers accompanying the pill, and other forms of birth control as well as the limitations in effectiveness. Many couples, perhaps moved by an ecological spirit, seem anxious to discover "nature's way" and respect it. Surprisingly, many parents who disagree with the Church on this issue want Church teaching presented to their children nevertheless. Of course, catechists representing the Church would be irresponsible to do anything less.

1. God is the creator of each individual person and the author and creator of marriage.

The nature of marriage and its purposes have been established by God. Marriage is both a vocation and a mission: a vocation in that a person is called by God to the married state and a mission in that the couple is sent, that is, given a responsibility and a ministry to carry out in marriage.

Conjugal love (or married love) has its origins in God who is love. The Second Vatican Council stated:

> Authentic married love is caught up into divine love and is governed and enriched by Christ's redeeming power and the saving activity of the Church, so that this love may lead the spouses to God with powerful effect and may aid and strengthen them in the sublime office of being a father or a mother. For this reason Christian spouses have a special sacrament by which they are fortified and receive a kind of consecration in the duties and dignity of their state (Constitution on the Church in the Modern World, no. 48).

Christ abundantly blesses the married love of Christians. Such love is modeled after His union with the Church. As God made Himself present to His people in the Old Testament through a covenant of love and fidelity, so now the Lord Jesus comes into the lives of married Christians through the Sacrament of Matrimony. A Christian couple is guaranteed the power and the presence of Jesus in their community of love.

Conjugal love is different from other loves in that it is founded on the vow made before God. In making this vow a man and a woman join themselves to each other by the covenant of irrevocable personal consent. Spouses promise to love, even should they not feel friendship between them. Such love is possible. One can love another without being loved in return. The marriage can continue to exist even when love goes one direction only, that is, from one spouse to the other, and not returned. Spouses hope their love will grow into a deep friendship, that is, that it will become a strong mutually affectionate love with God's help.

It is somewhat difficult for us in our culture and tradition to realize that for centuries in many societies people did not marry from love. Their marriages were arranged by their parents, or they decided to get married for reasons other than affectionate love between them. Conjugal love is founded upon a promise.

2. Christian marriage is "a communion of beings" collaborating with God in the generation and education of children.
Pope Paul VI, in *Humanae Vitae,* spoke of the four characteristics of conjugal love; namely, human, total, faithful, and fruitful.

Conjugal love is first of all fully human. It is both of the senses and of the spirit. It is not merely instinct nor merely feeling but is also a free act of the will. Husband and wife become one heart and one spirit, a truly human communion.

Conjugal love is total, that is, it is a special form of friendship in which husband and wife generously share everything "without undue or selfish calculation." In Christian marriage each partner is called to love the other without limit and unconditionally, that is, strictly for the other, without placing any conditions upon that love. Conjugal love is faithful and exclusive until death. On their wedding day bride and groom intend an exclusiveness which will last until death.

Finally, conjugal love is fruitful (fecund) in that it does not achieve its fullness in the communion between husband and wife but is meant rather to extend itself in the raising up of new lives. Vatican II taught "by their nature, the institution of matrimony itself and conjugal love are ordained for the procreation and education of children, and find in them their ultimate crown" (Church in the Modern World, no. 48).

3. The Church teaches that the unitive and procreative purposes are both essentially important and necessary.
Couples are called to be responsive and responsible to both of these purposes. The Christian spouse must strive to be responsible to each of the two essential purposes, which are inseparable from each other. Furthermore, these two purposes do not preclude other purposes, such as, economic and mutual help.

4. Christian couples carry out their responsibility to the unitive purpose by being faithful to their commitment, by tenderness and affection, by companionship and a common life, and by growing in their "communion of being."
Sometimes it happens that husband and wife are so involved in raising their children that they neglect their own relationship. It may come as a surprise to them, once their children all leave home and they are alone with each other, to find out that they are "strangers." It is important that throughout marriage, even while the children are growing up and demanding so much of their time, they do not neglect the relationship between them.

The unitive purpose has a certain priority in their relationship. Remembering anniversaries, birthdays, and noticing the special needs of the other are some important ways a husband or wife attends to the unitive purpose.

5. They carry out their responsibility to the procreative purpose by being open and responsible to life.
Should their love be blessed with the gift of children, the married couple must bring them up responsibly. There is a certain readiness that is necessary before a husband and a wife can procreate and educate children responsibly. The encyclical Humanae Vitae points to various aspects which need to be considered if a couple is to be responsible in parenting. One is the biological. This means the couple should know and respect the biological functions by which they give life to another human being. Secondly, the couple should realize that instinct or passion (their emotional life) are subject to the reason and will. In addition there are certain physical, economic, psychological, and social aspects which must be attended to and responded to if the couple is to be responsible.

To be responsible parents, the spouses must realize and fulfill their obligations and duties as parents. They need to be aware of their mission as responsible parents, a mission which includes procreation and education. Husband and wife are called procreators because it is God who immediately creates the human soul of the baby generated by their union. The second part of the mission of parents is to educate the child. The Vatican Council stated: "graced with the dignity and office of fatherhood and motherhood, parents will energetically acquit themselves of a duty which devolves primarily on them, namely education and especially religious education" (Church in the Modern World, no. 48).

6. The Church does not establish an ideal or "right number" of children.

The Council stated that couples should consider several factors in helping to determine the size of their families.

a. Couples need to consider both their own welfare and that of their children.

b. Couples need to reckon with both the material and spiritual condition of the times as well as their own state in life.

c. Couples need to consider the interests of the family group, of temporal society, and of the Church itself.

The Council went on to say that parents should ultimately make the judgment of the size of their family in the sight of God. A decade or two ago it was common in Catholic circles to feel somewhat pressured toward large families. Today, the opposite is true—Catholics experience a pressure in society which suggests a limit of two children per family. The Church's teaching is that the size of family is a personal judgment made in the sight of God by the couple. "Among the married couples who thus fulfill their God-given mission, special mention should be made of those who after prudent reflection and common decision courageously undertake the proper upbringing of a large number of children" (Church in the Modern World, no. 50). In making their decision spouses "should be aware that they cannot proceed arbitrarily, but must always be governed according to a conscience dutifully conformed to the divine law itself, and should be submissive toward the Church's teaching office, which authentically interprets that law in the light of the gospel."

7. Some couples seem to approach "having a family" with a very precise timetable, and a rigid determination as to exactly "how many" children they plan.

They leave little, if any, room for the unexpected or unplanned pregnancy, and seem to have little recognition of the mystery which life necessarily entails. Christian couples must be ready to accept the gift of life when and in whatever form it is given—twins, triplets, miscarriage, Downs Syndrome, healthy baby or sickly. The same is true of any unplanned pregnancy. Once life begins, it has a claim on its parents for reverent treatment and a proper rearing. Many are the parents who worked through feelings of disappointment at the news of an unplanned pregnancy to feelings of joy and acceptance. No child has to be unwanted.

8. Couples use various methods to regulate conception, sometimes to begin a pregnancy and other times to avoid a pregnancy.

The Church's teaching holds that the conjugal act, that is, sexual intercourse as an act of mutual committed love, is a gift of God with two meanings or purposes, unitive and procreative. The encyclical *Humanae Vitae* declares that "each and every marriage act must remain open to the transmission of life." This teaching rejects artificial methods of birth regulation which close off the couple to a possible conception during the woman's fertile time.

Two methods which are compatible with the Church's teaching contained in *Humanae Vitae* are the ovulation method, which employs mucus as an indicator of fertility, and the symptothermic method, which employs the mucus together with the temperature symptom as an indicator of fertility. It should be noted that these two methods are called "natural" because neither of them artificially closes off the conjugal act to a possible pregnancy. It should also be noted that neither of these methods is the so-called rhythm method.

9. Abstinence is a necessary part of every life.

At certain times, for example, due to the necessities and demands of work, business, pregnancy, or of travel, couples will have to abstain from sexual relations. When abstinence is difficult, the spouses should remember God's promise to be with them in the Sacrament of Marriage. Abstinence serves as a positive up-builder of conjugal love. It is founded upon reverence for God's will in creation.

LIST OF TERMS

Abstinence	Doing without; self-restraint, self-discipline.
Conception	Union of sperm and ovum which results in new life.
Contraceptives	Means and devices used to keep the woman from becoming pregnant. Most commonly used are: the pill, intrauterine devices (IUD), foams, jellies, diaphragms, and condoms.
Fertility	Ability to generate a child. Male and female must be fertile if a child is to be conceived and born of their union (opposite of *sterility*).
Mutuality	Sharing of sentiments between persons; agreement; sharing in common; reciprocal.
Natural Family Planning	Practice of spacing pregnancies according to an informed awareness of a woman's fertility.
Procreative Purpose	God's invitation to human persons to share in the creation of new life by the procreation and education of the child. Catholic tradition teaches that a man and woman are instrumental in God's creation of a new human life.
Responsible Parenthood	Moral accountability as mother and father. The parents of a child respond adequately to the moral requirements and necessities of being parents, fulfilling the procreative purpose of marriage.
Unitive Purpose	Mutual love and sharing of the two spouses.

12 Respect for Human Life

Dr. Smith warned her that the baby would be born crippled and probably retarded. Even so, Georgia and her husband, Vince, were determined to accept life however it came. And so Jason was born, a few weeks early and as the doctor predicted. His handicaps seemed easier to accept, somehow, having been forewarned.

He had been a good baby, easy to satisfy. He wore the corrective braces without much resistance, and the rest of the family had grown to love him deeply, especially Bobby and Terri, the oldest of the clan. Though they never discussed it explicitly, Georgia and Vince sensed that Jason was drawing the whole family into a tight and beautiful unit.

Looking ahead, Georgia could see more difficult times. Decisions, complex and sensitive, would soon have to be made. Could Jason handle "mainstreaming" or should he attend a school for special education? As he got bigger, how would the family manage the transportation? When the older children moved on to college in two and three years, who would help take care of him? protect him from cruelty and insensitivity?

Whispering a prayer, Georgia dismissed the questions. Her face became noticeably relaxed, and her shoulders dropped an inch. Jason was calling her into his room in his own special way. He was probably ready to sleep and wanted the lights out—but not before a reassuring embrace

and a stuttered "Good night." Since Vince had called to say
he was working late, she did the evening ritual alone
tonight.

When the first test-tube baby was born, Pope John Paul I expressed public greetings of welcome and blessing. At the same time, he challenged the morality and rightness of the method used to conceive the child. Unlike premarital pregnancies which have been with us probably throughout human history, test-tube babies are twentieth-century developments. In both instances, even though the circumstances surrounding the conception may be morally objectionable, once human life is begun it has a claim upon all other humans to respect its dignity and basic human rights.

New moral issues dealing with human life are being raised continually as scientists discover more keys to unlock the mysteries of nature. The issues are rarely simple. Are scientists going too far? How do we even go about resolving the question of what is "too far," to say nothing about the specific issues themselves?

Concern for life at all ages and stages has been on the increase. Stimulated greatly by the legalization and large number of abortions in the U.S. and by a growing awareness of the rights of handicapped persons, the elderly, minority groups, the hungry and other oppressed or deprived peoples, many clergy and lay persons have committed themselves to improving the quality of life for all.

At the heart of life concerns is the basic sense of morality being severely challenged by some of the prevailing winds of the day. Though I am aware of no studies explaining the moral mind-set of youth suicides, my experience suggests that a major cause is the "do your own thing" philosophy. Many today follow the maxim that "It's his life. He can do what he wants with it."

Applied to self, this approach to life holds one accountable to no one beyond self, neither God, nor family, nor friend. Christian youth have a right to better and firmer guidance than the current secular sources are giving them. No one but God has an absolute right over life. Our traditional wisdom and teaching states loudly and clearly that every person is accountable to the Creator for life. We do not have the right to do what we please even with life that we call "my own."

1. Life is a gift and a responsibility.

As a gift, life is something which is not merited nor acquired by works. Life is freely given by God, not something required of God, nor something God owed to anyone. From conception to death life's value is never lost. At every moment it is worthwhile and worthy of reverence and respect. Christian parents appreciate life as a gift, they value it and are open to handing it on. The first attitude one should have towards a gift is to be grateful for it and humble in its presence.

Life is also a responsibility. Responsibility means accountability, that is, the state of being answerable to another. With life it is none other than God to whom we are responsible. God puts a claim on those to whom He gives life. Those gifted with life are not only responsible for their own life but also responsible for other human life. The infant cannot be responsible for his or her life, and at times neither can the sick, the elderly, nor the handicapped. These human lives call for a response from the mature and able. They need to be cared for by others. Being a baby or sick or aged or disabled does not forfeit the right to be cared for, the right to live. God puts the claim on the able human being to care for these lives.

2. It is a fundamental Christian teaching that we are but stewards and caretakers of the gifts given us by the Creator.

Every human being has an inalienable right to life and the right to be reverenced and respected as a human person. It is morally wrong to discriminate for any reason whatever, whether a person be handicapped or of a different race or color or sex or age or creed. Laws must protect the rights of people and the goods that belong to people. Laws must reflect the moral order. Pope John XXIII in the great encyclical *Pacem in Terris* stated:

> Any human society, if it is to be well-ordered and productive, must lay down as a foundation this principle, namely, that every human being is a person, that is, his or her nature is endowed with intelligence and free will. By virtue of this, humans have rights and duties of their own, flowing directly and simultaneously from their very nature. These rights are therefore universal, inviolable, and inalienable (no. 9).
>
> . . . Every person has the right to life, to bodily integrity, and to the means which are necessary and suitable for the proper development of life (no. 11).
>
> It is generally accepted today that the common good is best safeguarded when personal rights and duties are guaranteed. The chief concern of civil authorities must therefore be to ensure that these rights are recognized, respected, coordinated, defended and promoted, and that each individual is enabled to perform his or her duties more easily. For "to safeguard the inviolable rights of the human person, and to facilitate the performance of his or her duties, is the principal duty of every public authority" (no. 60).

3. It is the teaching of the Catholic Church that human life begins at the moment of fertilization.

When the male sperm unites with the female ovum a new human life begins. This new life has its required number of chromosomes, 46, containing all its basic organic inheritance from both parents. The human being's potential is established at that point; all the new life needs is development. The fertilized ovum represents a complete human genetic package. This newly conceived life is unique, differing genetically from its parents as a unique combination of genes. The Church's Declaration on Abortion states: "From the time that the ovum is fertilized, a life is begun which is neither that of the father nor of the mother; it is rather the life of a new human being with his or her growth."

From this teaching it is clear why Catholics cannot and do not accept as moral the ruling of the U.S. Supreme Court in January, 1973, legalizing abortions. If we believe that life begins at conception, then this new life has the same right to protection as any human life.

4. Three serious sins against life are considered in this chapter, namely, abortion, infanticide, and suicide.
This list is not to deny other sins against life; for example, negligence, child battering, self-mutilation, injustice, prejudice, starvation, and others. But these three seem to have special relevance for a catechesis in sexuality for youth and their parents.

Abortion is the deliberate ending of an unborn human life. More precisely, induced abortion is the "deliberate destruction of a fetus before viability" (from the *New Catholic Encyclopedia,* 1967, Vol. 1, under "abortion"). When someone makes a decision and attempts or succeeds to end the life of an unborn child, this is abortion. Sometimes an unborn life is ended without the deliberation and decision of a person. (In medical terminology this is called a spontaneous abortion; usually we refer to this as a miscarriage.) Spontaneous abortion happens when the uterus, for natural reasons, goes into labor early in pregnancy. Why this happens is not always known, but usually the developing baby has died because of some abnormality, and the mother's body rejects the dead embryo. A miscarriage is not an abortion in the usual sense and is not morally wrong.

Abortion which is the deliberate ending of life is done in four common ways. They are (1) dilation and currettage (D and C), (2) suction, (3) hysterotomy, and (4) saline poisoning. It will be important to point out that "D and C" is the term also given a procedure commonly prescribed by doctors for the removal of tissue in the uterus by a method of dilation and currettage. Since this involves no developing embryo, it is not an abortion. The "D and C" which is an abortion method removes the developing embryo from the lining of the uterus. The suction method using a vacuum apparatus can be used until the thirteenth week of pregnancy. The hysterotomy is similar to a caesarean section and is used after the fourteenth week of pregnancy. The saline method which employs an injection of a highly concentrated salt solution is used after the fifteenth week of pregnancy. Other methods of abortion are being developed.

5. The direct destruction of the unborn child in abortion is always morally wrong.

Catholics are called to witness to the sanctity of life by respecting and defending human life before birth as well as afterward. It would be well to quote a segment of the pastoral message of the administrative committee of the National Conference of Catholic Bishops. This letter was issued February 13, 1973, shortly after the Supreme Court decision. The Bishops said . . .

> . . . We reject the opinion of the United States Supreme Court as erroneous, unjust, and immoral. Because of our responsibilities as authentic religious leaders and teachers, we make the following pastoral applications:
>
> (1) Catholics must oppose abortion as an immoral act. No one is obliged to obey any civil law that may require abortion.
>
> (2) Abortion is and has always been considered a serious violation of God's law. Those who obtain an abortion, those who persuade others to have an abortion, and those who perform the abortion procedures are guilty of breaking God's law. Moreover, in order to emphasize the special evil

of abortion, under Church law, those who undergo or perform an abortion place themselves in a state of excommunication.

(3) As tragic and sweeping as the Supreme Court decision is, it is still possible to create a pro-life atmosphere in which all, and notably physicians and health care personnel, will influence their peers to see a value in all human life, including that of the unborn child during the entire course of pregnancy. We hope that doctors will retain an ethical concern for the welfare of both the mother and the unborn child, and will not succumb to social pressure in performing abortions.

(4) We urge the legal profession to articulate and safeguard the rights of fathers of unborn children, rights that have not been upset by this Supreme Court opinion.

(5) We praise the efforts of pro-life groups and many other concerned Americans and encourage them to:

(a) Offer positive alternatives to abortion for distressed pregnant women;

(b) Pursue protection for institutions and individuals to refuse on the basis of conscience to engage in abortion procedures;

(c) Combat the general permissiveness legislation can engender;

(d) Assure the most restrictive interpretation of the Court's opinion at the state legislative level;

(e) Set in motion the machinery needed to assure legal and constitutional conformity to the basic truth that the unborn child is a "person" in every sense of the term from the time of conception.

Bringing about a reversal of the Supreme Court's decision and achieving respect for unborn human life in our society will require unified and persistent efforts. But we must begin now—in our churches, schools, and homes, as well as in the larger civic community—to instill reverence for life at all stages. We take as our mandate the words of the Book of Deuteronomy:

"I set before you life or death. . . . Choose life, then, that you and your descendents may live. . . ."

6. Infanticide is the deliberate taking of the life of the newborn and very young child.

Infanticide has always been seen as a horrible and vicious immoral act. One of the most renowned historical commissions of this sin was at the time of Jesus' birth, when King Herod tried to kill Jesus by slaying all of the infant boys in Bethlehem under two years old. This unspeakable crime has been done periodically throughout history on a massive scale, but it has also been done individually.

Infanticide is important to discuss at this time of history since, with the legality of abortion and the pressures toward euthanasia, more and more consideration is being given to the right of adults over the life of an infant. One doctor has suggested that life should be said to begin three days after birth so that parents might be allowed time to decide whether or not the child's life should be maintained. If they wanted a girl and got a boy, they may want to reconsider and not accept the boy. Or if the child was born with a defect of one kind or other, which after three days of consideration they decided was significant enough to warrant rejection of this baby, they would have the legal right to do so. One need not be very imaginative to see the tremendous harm such a procedure would bring upon society. The Church teaches that infanticide is seriously sinful.

7. Suicide, the intentional and voluntary taking of one's own life, is contrary to the Christian stance toward life.

Suicide is one of the top three killers of youth in America today. It represents a terrible suffering for the families involved and an extremely difficult and complex trend to analyze and assess. It seems to strike well-functioning families as well as the disfunctioning. Given its prevalence and uncertainty, open discussion among parents and teachers is certainly warranted.

One factor is presented here as a possible contributor to suicide's prevalence; namely, the common attitude that "It's his or her life; the person can do with it whatever he or she wants!" A story may illustrate more clearly the powerful impact that this attitude may have on our youth. Some time ago a young woman visited a counselor because her parents insisted she see someone. The parents were concerned because their daughter, sixteen years old, an occasional pot-user, a high school dropout, but otherwise an apparently "normal" teen-ager, had talked about committing suicide several months earlier. In the course of the counseling session, the discussion settled upon the girl's feeling that she was not obliged to help her friends who were damaging their own lives by excessive chemical use and dangerous driving. "It's their life," she insisted. "They can do with it anything they want!"

Applying this to her own life, the counselor realized that she felt she could do anything she wanted with her own life, including ending it. (The counselor noted later that this is one of the destructive outcomes of the "Do your own thing" philosophy.) In other words, this person did not understand that God is the giver of life, that she is responsible to God for her own life, and that she did not have the right to do anything she wanted with it. Her life is not her own to give or to take. There was no moral basis for this young woman to prevent her from destroying life itself.

The basic Christian stance towards life is that it is a gift from God and that we are all responsible to God for the life we have been given. This moral norm may not be enough to answer all the emotional and cultural factors involved in the suicide phenomenon among youth, but it certainly is an important one, and one that ought not to be overlooked.

Experts and agencies can be utilized to assist adults in the prevention and care of suicide-prone persons.

8. Generally, our society attempts to respect life and promote it.

Our government tries to pass legislation and establish institutions which assist human life at every stage and in every condition. Laws and governmental agencies which promote justice for the oppressed respect life. Developing an attitude of respect and reverence for life must be part of the air we breathe. The Church and many other private institutions and agencies have committed themselves to respecting life. The hospices where patients dying of cancer can die with dignity are a manifestation of the Church's commitment to life. Homes for orphaned and parentless children, asylums and institutions for lepers, homes for runaway teenagers, refuges for battered women, halfway houses for recovering alcoholics and former inmates of prisons—all these manifest a respect for life. Efforts to assist the deaf, the blind, and the mentally and physically handicapped show respect for life. Those who assist refugees show reverence for life.

Young people should be encouraged to get involved in the promotion of life. They can do so in a variety of ways. They are not too young to write letters to members of Congress and to others who have some responsibility for society's protection of human life. They also can benefit greatly from visiting institutions which nurture and protect life, for example, institutions operated by the Church for persons with problem pregnancies, and the elderly and the troubled. With some guidance young teenagers can get to know the handicapped and elderly. They will better come to respect life and promote it to the degree that they appreciate it as a gift and a responsibility.

9. Churches provide a comprehensive program of assistance to unmarried pregnant women and the fathers, as well as assistance to families of unmarried parents.
Catholic social service agencies offer service also to young married couples who have concerns relating to pregnancies. They do pregnancy testing, give help in obtaining whatever medical care is necessary, make arrangements for education, and will help the family find living quarters. Birthright chapters have been established throughout the nation to help problem pregnancies. These and other agencies and people are available to help.

LIST OF TERMS

Abortion	Deliberate destruction of the unborn.
	a. Suction abortion (drawing the developing embryo from the uterus using a vacuum method).
	b. D and C abortion (using a surgical instrument to scrape the wall of the uterus to remove the fetus).
	c. Saline solution (using a poisonous salt solution and inserting it into the protective covering called the "amniotic sac;" the fetus dies after intaking the solution).
	d. Hysterotomy abortion (the unborn baby is removed from the uterus, by making a surgical incision in the abdomen of the mother, and is left to die).
Caesarian Section	Surgical operation for delivering a baby by cutting through the mother's abdominal uterine walls.
Euthanasia	Killing persons who are suffering or considered useless.
Fetus	Offspring in the womb from the end of the third month of pregnancy until birth. (Prior to the end of the third month it is called an *embryo*.)
Incest	Sexually abusive activity between persons so closely related that they are forbidden by law to marry.
Infanticide	Deliberate destruction of a newborn or young child.
Judaeo-Christian Ethic	Right morality according to Jewish and Christian traditions.
Murder	Act of directly killing a human being.
Neonate	The newborn.
Rape	Sexual intercourse without consent; usually a male forcing intercourse upon a female.
Suicide	Act of taking one's own life voluntarily and intentionally.

13 Developing a Christian Conscience

An hour to go before the party's end. Barb felt trapped. She wished she had declined rather than accepted Brad's offer to take her home. She had accepted the invitation before she happened into a conversation that all but demolished her once shiny image of him. She didn't know whether to believe the stories about his sexual appetite and find another way home, or chance it.

Minutes ticked by slowly. It was the longest hour of her life. Back and forth she argued within herself. Should she call home and ask Dad to pick her up? She could pretend to be sick and leave early. That seemed dishonest and a coward's way out. She felt like asking Brad outright whether she would be safe with him. Suddenly, she grasped his arm and blurted out in a loud whisper, "Brad, I'm not into sex. Will you take me right home?"

He seemed to delight in the question, responding with a sinister smile, a pat on the thighs, and an inaudible "yes." Trying not to lose her composure, Barb felt betrayed and angry. She wanted to kick him. Controlling herself, she brushed his hands away and walked to the phone. She decided the stories about Brad must be true. No way was she going to put herself at a disadvantage with a man she couldn't trust. She dialed, Dad answered; he'd be there in fifteen minutes.

The pendulum is blamed for excesses in either direction. It's also used as an explanation for constant change, for unplanned and apparently inevitable indiscretions and for the general unrest and instability of a society at practically any point in time. People seem to sense the pendulum's swing to the extreme and when it has begun its return.

If the '50s were the time of legalism, institutional loyalties, and objective standards, the late '60s and early '70s were a time of intuition, free-spirits, and absolute relativity. "Let your conscience be your guide" meant one thing in the earlier period, and something totally other in the latter. The '80s may well be characterized by something in between.

Life is neither all black nor white, that is, clear-cut and well-defined, nor all gray, that is, necessarily in a constant state of confusion and fuzziness. There are blacks and whites but not as many as the '50s would have it; there are grays, but not as many as the '60s and '70s would have it.

So it goes with the concept of sin: over-played at one time and under-played at another. The '80s seem to be defining a new and more sensible balance. The pendulum is swinging back toward middle. Pulled one direction or the other in all of this is the individual conscience. Peering within and looking outside oneself, the sincere person searches for the truth that liberates, that sets free. Whether or not one possesses the truth, conscience makes its judgments—not always with the best information and insight, but judging anyway, because judge it must.

1. Conscience is the intellect making a judgment about the rightness or wrongness of a particular action.
Conscience is the judgment a person arrives at after applying moral principles to a proposed action. Conscience is not something outside or separate from oneself. It is not an imaginative figure standing on one's shoulder whispering inspirational thoughts. Neither is conscience a faculty or power separate from the mind or intellect.

The Second Vatican Council document on the Church in the Modern World states:

> In the depths of his conscience, man detects a law which he does not impose upon himself, but which holds him to obedience. Always summoning him to love good and avoid evil, the voice of conscience when necessary speaks to his heart: do this, shun that. For man has in his heart a law written by God; to obey it is the very dignity of man; according to it he will be judged. Conscience is the most secret core and sanctuary of a man. There he is alone with God, whose voice echoes in his depths. In a wonderful manner conscience reveals that law which is fulfilled by love of God and neighbor. In fidelity to conscience, Christians are joined with the rest of men in the search for truth, and for the genuine solution to the numerous problems which arise in the life of individuals and from social relationship. Hence, the more correct conscience holds sway, the more persons and groups turn aside from blind choice and strive to be guided by the objective norms of morality (no.16).

2. In every person's heart God has written basic laws.
Those who follow Christ interpret those basic laws as Jesus did, appreciating values as Jesus did, making choices to live as Jesus did. A Christian conscience, then, is one in tune with the values and principles of Jesus. St. Paul challenges us to "put on the mind of Christ . . . ," that is, to take on the values and perspective of Jesus. Blessed with this model, the Christian person makes moral judgments in the light of Jesus' teachings and example. God speaks to every human person through creation and to some—those endowed with Christian faith—God speaks in a special way. As children of God, Christians are endowed by God with the capacity within faith to act in harmony with His mind and will.

Sometimes a person misjudges the morality of a situation, calling something evil, which is truly good, or vice versa. For example, teenagers who drink to excess, even to the point of unconsciousness, sometimes mistakenly believe that this type of activity is not morally wrong. The general society in which they live may put no moral prohibition on drunkenness as sinful, and the commonness of the occurrence among their peers may lead them to believe that drunkenness is a morally neutral act. Hence, they see nothing wrong with getting drunk. Their conscience is in error. They do not rightly appreciate the value of life, or health, or safety, or responsibility for life and safety. A correct conscience would appreciate the irresponsibility of the action and judge it to be wrong.

3. The moral life has several components: ideals, values, norms, laws, and freedom.

Ideals are the values I hold as important in my life. They are good in themselves (objectively valid) and also important to me (subjectively worthwhile). There is an objective order to be perceived by us. This is the order established by the Creator. This moral order is for our good, always for our perfection in God's design. The subjective worth is what I perceive in each ideal or value and represents my convictions towards them.

Values are expressed in moral norms or moral principles. These norms are objective, God-given, either revealed or written in our hearts. For example, truth is a value and it is expressed in a norm such as, "Be honest in your relationships, do not lie or deceive." A loving relationship is a value, and is expressed in a norm such as, "Be kind to others as you would have them be kind to you." Behind every norm there is a value.

Objective norms should form our ideals and our consciences. These norms are needed to be flesh on the bare bones of ideals. The ideal by itself is usually difficult to grasp. For example, the ideal "love" is so general that it may be misinterpreted or misunderstood without objective norms. Without norms and, further, the next step of specification, namely, laws, it is very difficult to apply ideals to everyday living.

Laws are formulations of moral norms and the term *law* has many meanings. Moral laws guide our actions which deal with moral right or wrong. At its deepest level, the moral law is written in our hearts. It is the basic sense that one ought to do good and avoid evil. Jesus introduced Christian love as the new law, a general guiding principle that should direct our lives and govern our actions.

But what about more specific human laws, for example, those dealing with justice in business, care of offspring, care of health and property, responsible use of sex, honesty in relationships? Such human laws are good and necessary for society, and they assist individuals in making many decisions. However, the laws are not themselves the values. They flow from values and they protect values. They must be seen in relationship to the values which give them their meaning. People today are very conscious of values, and their attitudes towards laws can be strengthened positively by a deeper awareness and appreciation of the values which underpin the laws. This is an important responsibility of catechesis.

God reveals to us in Jesus Christ who we are and how we are to live as brothers and sisters of Jesus and as children of God. Who are we? God's children. How are we to live? As Jesus did. We are called to holiness, and the only commandment Jesus gave us to follow is the commandment of Christian love. "Love one another as I have loved you." This is not easy. The National Catechetical Directory reminds us:

> Nor may our decisions be arbitrary, for "good" and "bad," "right" and "wrong" are not simply whatever we choose to make them. On the contrary, there are moral values and norms which are absolute and never to be disregarded or violated by anyone in any situation. Fidelity to moral values and norms of this kind can require the heroism seen in the lives of the saints and the deaths of martyrs (NCD, no. 101).

4. The starting point for moral judgment is an appreciation of values, norms, and laws.

This means an individual has a basic sense of the worth of genuine values. Along with this is a sense of the relationship between norms, laws, and values.

The first step in the process of making moral judgments is deliberation. In this step a person reflects on the situation, considering, deliberating, and generally doing some searching. Another aspect of deliberation is counsel. A person can benefit greatly from the experience of others, if he or she would seek the counsel and advice of others. Especially can this be so for the Christian who seeks counsel from the Church. The Church has a long memory and a rich storehouse of experience. In addition, prayer and the sacramental life of the Church have a role to play in deliberation. Prayer opens up a person to the presence and word of God. The sacraments present a religious and Christian focus to life, being instruments of God's presence and power in the world.

The process of deliberation may take a short or long time, depending on the significance of the decision being made, the availability and adequacy of information, the pressure of time, and one's commitment to values. Someone who is strongly committed to a particular value will not need much time to make decisions in which that value is threatened. A person who is unsure where he or she stands relative to a particular value may need a long time to sort things out and make some decision.

5. The second step in the process of making judgments is the actual judgment of conscience.

Deliberation prepares one to make the judgment that, to do this is right, to do that is wrong. Oftentimes we speak in this vein: my conscience tells me that stealing is wrong. To take this money from my employer would be an act of stealing and therefore morally wrong. Note that I have not yet acted. I have only made a judgment that for me to act in a certain way is morally wrong. Conscience is the judgment I make about the rightness or wrongness of an action.

Sin is the deliberate rejection of a person's role as a child of God and a member of His people. We sin when we knowingly and deliberately disobey God's command to love Him, other people, and ourselves in a morally right way. When we sin, we turn aside or even turn away from our God, turning our backs rather than our faces towards Him. Sin always deals death. A grave offense or serious sin radically disrupts our relationship with God and places us in danger of everlasting death. Less serious offenses impair our relationship with God and can lead us to more serious sin.

Guilt is the feeling of responsibility or remorse for some real or imagined offense or sin. Guilt is necessary and good if it corresponds to the truth of a situation. Guilt is misplaced and not good if it does not correspond to the reality of the situation and if it leads to negative and destructive outcomes. It is important that genuine guilt be recognized and responded to in ways that lead to true sorrow, growth and development.

6. After I make a judgment that an act is right or wrong then it is up to me to do it or not.
This is the third step. If I decide to act contrary to the dictates of my conscience, then my action is immoral and I commit sin. For example, if I value honesty and I realize that the clerk has made a ten-dollar error in my favor, and my conscience tells me that honesty requires that I return the ten dollars and I deliberately choose not to, I have gone against my conscience. I have committed an immoral act defying both my values and my judgment of conscience. If I had chosen to return the money in accord with my conscience, I would have done a morally good act.

Finally, I may do the action decided. If I go against the judgment of conscience, I commit sin. To act in accord with my conscience is to act in a morally right manner. Doing the good actually helps a person develop conscience. One learns good by doing good. A person develops a right conscience by doing what is right. It is not enough to know the truth—a person must love it and do it.

7. Jesus is the key to the formation of a Christian conscience.
What did Jesus love, how did he live, what was important and of value to him? The life and teachings of Jesus Christ revealed to us the will of the Father and ultimate purpose of humankind. The conscience of Jesus was one with the Father. He acted according to the Father's will, and he shows us the way to the Father. "I am the way, the truth, and the life" (John 14:6).

Jesus is the sacrament of God, the sign of the Father's love for us, and the embodiment of the Father's plan for us. Jesus saw what was of real and genuine value in the world. He used the good things of nature and taught us to respect and accept them. Jesus shows us the way to our own human fulfillment and our fulfillment as children of the Father. He gives us practical guides for the formation of our consciences and the determination of our personal ideals and values. Jesus proposed moral ideals not as impossible and unreachable guides, but as norms by which we are to live. What is more, He is present in His spirit to strengthen us and enable us to live a life worthy of the calling we have received (cf Ephesians 4:1). Jesus is the first source in the development of a Christian conscience.

8. A second source for the development of a Christian conscience is the Church, the Body of Christ living in the present, imbued with God's own Spirit dwelling within and speaking to our hearts.
"Wherever two or three are gathered in my name, there I am in the midst of them" (Matthew 18:20). The official teaching of the Church has a special place among the ways that God teaches us about the moral life. That teaching binds the individual Catholic conscience and is a sure guide to true charity for a disciple of Christ. We believe that Jesus did not abandon His people but continues to guide us and to share His spirit with us in the Church.

The National Catechetical Directory states:

The Holy Father, and the Bishops in communion with him have been anointed by the Holy Spirit to be the official and authentic teachers of Christian life. For Jesus "established His Church by sending forth the Apostles as He himself had been sent by the Father. (cf John 20, 21) He willed that their successors, namely, the bishops should be shepherds in His Church even to the consummation of the world" (NCD, no. 104).

9. The Christian conscience becomes more in tune with the mind and heart of Christ as liturgical, sacramental, scriptural, and prayer experiences have their effect.

Liturgy and sacraments are primary and indispensable instructors shaping a Christian mentality and strengthening a person to accomplish what is impossible by human strength alone.

Scripture is an essential source of information and inspiration for the development of a Christian conscience. It contains the wisdom of God's people and was written under the inspiration of the Holy Spirit.

A life of personal prayer and union with God also shapes conscience. In prayer, where people grow in knowledge and love of Christ and commitment to His service, the power of God transforms the Christian into a clearer image of the Father. As the union of hearts becomes more complete, so does the action of the human heart reflect the desires of the divine.

LESSON 13   LIST OF TERMS

Conscience
Intellect making a judgment about the rightness or wrongness of a particular action.

Christian Conscience
One in tune with the values and principles of Jesus.

Guidance
Assistance given or sought which helps a person discover the moral good.

Guilt
Awareness of having done something morally wrong, with its accompanying sadness.

Ideal
Values a person holds as important in life.

Laws
Rational and permanent norms for human behavior enacted and promulgated by proper authority for the sake of the common good.

Moral Act, Good Act
Any human activity done in accord with the moral law in good conscience.

Moral Judgment
Judgment in accord with the moral law and in good conscience; true judgment.

Moral Norm
Standard or criterion expressing right behavior. It expresses the good as intended by the Creator (natural moral law).

Responsibility
Capacity to be accountable for one's personal behavior in relation to self, others, and God.

Sin
Deliberate refusal to live according to God's plan as one knows it. It is going against one's conscience.

Value
Something worthwhile in itself and hence prized or esteemed. It is that which is held dear and considered of worth.

14 Facing Peer Pressure

Jim's parents were highly principled people, and they taught their children well. He knew their feelings about abortion, but what could he do? His friend, Kathy, was seriously considering it. Should he talk to her and try to convince her otherwise? After all, it wasn't his child. Maybe he shouldn't get involved.

The conversation did not go well with Kathy. She said she wasn't sure about abortion being wrong. She had already been to the clinic with her boyfriend, and abortion seemed like the simplest and best thing to do. Three girls she knew at school had abortions last year, and they told her it wasn't so bad.

Jim even tried to talk Kathy's boyfriend out of it, who admitted his belief that it was wrong; but he told Jim that it was Kathy's body, and he would support whatever decision she made. He said he had discussed the situation with a counselor at school, and the counselor seemed to think an abortion would be okay.

As a final effort, Jim asked Kathy to tell her parents about her pregnancy. She said she felt they wouldn't understand, and, besides, she didn't want to hurt them. They would be crushed, she told him, if they found out she had been sexually involved. Better they never know, she decided.

Jim felt like crying.

Gone is the day, it seems, when parents get much help from the neighbors in raising their children. In a recent conversation with friends, we recalled how fast the neighbors reported to our homes the misbehaviors they observed as we made our way home from school. Like the time my friend puffed on a cigarette one block from his house, and his mother greeted him at the door a few minutes later with a scolding for smoking. A neighbor called his mother. Our parents had lots of help, and we had a score of concerned adults parenting us.

Have you checked your neighborhood lately mid-day? In mine all the houses are empty. When Johnny and Jane leave school, they can hustle over to either home and have at least an hour or two of privacy. And no observing neighbors to report the rendezvous to their parents. Studies indicate that after-school hours are prime times for youthful adventures into sexual behavior. Prime time for vandalism is also after school.

Youth's own peers have become the dominant influence over youth's moral behavior, not only because of the development of a subculture among them, but also because Mom and Dad aren't present and parenting during much of their teen's leisure time.

One of my favorite quotes comes from a paperback I read in the '50s, the title of which I have since forgotten. The quote goes: "In trying to give our kids all the things we didn't have, are we failing to give them what we did have?"

One thing kids need more of today is adults who share their lives, their experience, and their parentlike concern for the "new crop" coming up. Parenting has never been solely the responsibility of parents, nor should it be. But neither should it be a role given over to youth's peers. A contribution the churches could make to youth ministry would be to help parents keep kids in families.

1. A peer is one who is an equal. Often the term applies to people who are of the same age grouping, or it designates those who are of the same professional or career category.
As used in this chapter the term applies to youth in their relationships to each other.

Whenever any group of people get together there is going to be some "pressure" present. "Group pressure" is the influence that one is subject to in relating with any group. It takes many forms, some of them verbal, some nonverbal. It can be positive or negative, constructive or destructive. It may be morally good or bad or even morally neutral, depending upon the nature of what is being promoted. At times, the pressure is very subtle and unnoticeable, at other times it can be very dominant and obvious. Sometimes peer pressure is the result of one person's influence; sometimes it is the result of a group's consensus.

2. Another way to analyze peer pressure is to list the values of the members of a group, especially those values which determine the major choices and decisions which group members make individually or collectively.
If most members of a group value sobriety, drunken behavior will not be acceptable within the group. This value will influence who will be allowed to join and who will remain with the group. It will also influence the direction of the group's activities.

Young people can be helped to sort out their lives by looking at the dominant and determining values of their peers. What value do their peers place on human dignity and worth, how do they value themselves, their families and friends? Does God have a real place in their lives? Is Church important to them? Is it important to them that they keep their promises, respect property, act with integrity and honesty, strive for wholeness? Do they value work and the product of work?

Who shapes the values of young people today and how are their values being formed? What values are being inculcated by their parents, Church, the media, school, and peers? Are they Christian values? Do young people themselves feel some responsibility for the values they are internalizing?

3. This book has dealt with life and family values from the viewpoint of the Catholic Christian community.
Most church communities today seem to be concerned about the valuing process of their children and youth. A major concern for many is the value system of youth which deals with life and family. Obviously, this includes all aspects of sexuality. What are the influences that are shaping the sexuality of youth? How much are they being affected by the songs they listen to, the television programs they watch, the example of the significant adults in their lives, their religious faith and experience?

The responsibility that adults feel toward the younger generation can appear overwhelming at times. Our example and witness to Christian values is never perfect and often seems woefully deficient. But, adults should not lose heart. We lose sight too easily of the good in our lives, and we can overlook the good in the lives of our young people. Wanting them to be perfect, perhaps, we concentrate on what might be, losing sight of what already is. They usually want what is right and what is best. They will learn from the experience of others and appreciate the helps they are given.

4. One of the greatest helps that is available to young people in living out life and family values is the support they receive from their families and from their Church.
Many youth today feel isolated and alone in their struggle with genuine values, especially Christian values. They appreciate ways in which they can receive encouragement and support.

Trends among their peers are sometimes negative and destructive. Youth need to know that there is an alternative which is better and which is available to them. Many Christian youth are finding support for their life and family values from prayer groups, Christian organizations, church youth groups and friendship with believing Christian adults. Many are greatly encouraged by the witness to Christian values given by young adults and youth workers they come to know.

Also very important in the shaping of values is the positive witness that youth give to each other. They have tremendous power in this regard with the high level of influence peer groups seem to have on one another. With power comes responsibility. One aim of this chapter is to help young people realize how important they are in the lives of others.

5. If it is true that peer pressure among youth is strong today, then the Reverence for Life and Family program would do well to help youth understand what it is, how it works and how they might respond responsibly to it.
The first response is the realization that no group should ever be allowed to take away the individual's responsibility. People are responsible for their lives. This includes the responsibility to be sure that the individual's freedom is neither destroyed nor impaired. Many times young people will find themselves pressured into doing things they really wouldn't choose to do. These experiences can teach them a lot about themselves. How they act in a group, how they allow themselves to be influenced by certain people, how they shrink from voicing their own opinions under certain conditions, how they allow certain leaders to determine directions or set patterns which they may not agree with, and so on. It is extremely important for youth to understand the dynamics of peer pressure and its effect on personal responsibility.

Secondly, young people can respond to peer pressure by realizing their own power and responsibility to either redirect it or lead it in the right direction from the beginning. Parents and teachers can help them to appreciate their own goodness and realize God's call to them to be living witnesses in their world.

6. Three inadequate guidelines, each faulty and misleading, are prevailing determiners of much sexual behavior.
Disregarding reason, faith, history, wisdom, collective conscience, and advice of elders, young people have committed themselves, as a generation, to following the statement, "If it feels good, do it." A popular song reinforcing this philosophy questions how something which "feels so good" can possibly be wrong. Feelings are not the whole story. Sometimes they help us do the moral good; other times they hinder us. Feelings may hinder us in two ways: by moving us to do wrong or by keeping us from doing what is right.

A second inadequate guide is the statement "As long as nobody gets hurt, it's okay." Part of the difficulty with this, especially for youth, is the disadvantage their age gives them. Life is not as simple as youth perceive it to be. It is characteristic of youth to be hasty, failing to see beyond the obvious. They are not as ready as adults are to admit potential dangers nor to recognize injuries.

A third inadequate guide common today is this: "As long as both agree, sex is okay." Although this has some merit—at least freedom is not violated—it fails to face a basic and essential aspect of moral behavior, namely, is it (whatever they are doing) morally right and good for the individuals involved? Two people can agree on anything. Is what they agree on a moral good?

7. Added to these three faulty maxims is the deeply felt impression that sex is for fun.
True, sex is pleasurable because God made it so. The purpose of sex is not to serve pleasure, but rather the purpose of sexual pleasure is to serve sex. Both its unitive and creative pleasure is to serve sex. Both its unitive and creative purposes are to be

served by the way a person enjoys as well as foregoes sexual pleasures.

8. Staging the contrast between the contemporary hedonistic approach and the counter-cultural Christian approach to sexual activity highlights their differences and conflicts.

	Current Culture Hedonistic Approach	Counter-culture Christian Approach
1. Ordinary purpose of sex	Pleasure	Procreation and loving union
2. Value desired from sexual activity	Pleasurable feelings achieved through genital expression, between caring persons unmarried or married, same sex or opposite, through oral and genital activity	Union of persons achieved through permanent commitment expressed in genital intercourse between faithful spouses, married, opposite sex
3. Attitudes promoted	Sex is for fun, for all age groups, in any state of life; make love by loving sex; contraceptive mentality	Sexual activity (intercourse and foreplay), including pleasure, is for married persons, not for children and youth, not for singles; sex expresses committed love
4. Potential dangers	Separates sex from responsibility; promotes sex-saturation; encourages genital liaisons without commitment; great "orgasm hunt"; excessive individualism	Separates pleasure from purpose of sex; develops a new puritanism

Hedonism tends to separate sex from responsibility, to promote genital emphasis, and to encourage genital liaisons without commitment.

9. Pressures on youth to be sexually active can be extremely subtle, pervasive, and very forceful.
One final aspect deserving our attention is the idea that "Everybody's doing it!" In some locales chastity and virginity have been given such a bad name by the pleasure-principle promoters that practitioners of these virtues and possessers of these qualities have been afraid to come out into the open. Only recently, it seems, has it been "Okay to say no."

In our home whenever we kids tried to justify something with the argument that "all the other kids are doing it," my dad always countered with, "If they all jump off the High Bridge, are you going to do it, too?" Majority morality is not the Christian way, but it remains a day-to-day challenge for Christians.

LESSON 14   LIST OF TERMS

Christian Values Values revealed by Jesus and held by His people.

Church (Roman Catholic) Those who believe in Jesus and are united with the Pope and the Catholic Bishops in the profession of faith, and in the celebration of the Eucharist and other Sacraments.

Counsel Advice. A person can benefit greatly from the experience of others.

Family Values That which is of essential worth to the institution of the family, e.g., marriage covenant, community of love, procreation, obedience, loyalty, mutual parenting.

Life Values That which is of essential worth to the existence of human life, e.g., wholeness, temperance, human dignity, fidelity, commitment, spirit of sacrifice.

Peer Person belonging to the same group (usually, age group).

Peer Pressure Influence one is subject to in relating to one's peers.

Support for Values Strength that comes from knowing and experiencing values held in common.

Witnessing Christian Values Showing by example the values held by Jesus and His people.

15 Life and Family Values

Jesse was fourteen and already a failure in his own eyes. Elton, his friend, and Nicki (short for Veronica), Jesse's sister, had both hassled him for experimenting with pot. For some reason, which Jesse couldn't figure out, they had this big thing on drugs, and he felt they were being hypocritical since they seemed to have no qualms about the abuse of alcohol.

Besides the nagging of Elton and Veronica, Jesse was occasionally bothered by a statement his dad made once, something to the effect that chemical abuse was similar to drinking gasoline or eating tacks; if God had wanted people to consume this stuff, He would have designed the plumbing to handle it! How harmful was pot anyway? A lot of the guys at school didn't seem hurt by it. Was he being stupid or wasn't he? Was it wrong, morally wrong, he wondered.

Wishing he had better answers, he stared straight at the ceiling one night in bed and began the most direct talk with God ever in his life. "OK Lord, tell me, what's wrong with marijuana? If it's so bad, why did you make it? And if what I'm doing is so wrong, why did You make me?" Jesse waited for the answers, as abruptly as he had blurted out the questions. Silence.

Then he thought he heard someone say, "Jesse, I love you. You are precious to me." More silence. Was his mind playing tricks; was he talking to himself? How do you know if it's God's voice or your own? "Precious to me," the voice said. "I am?" Jesse whispered back.

The battle for the future of Western civilization is engaged. It is a battle over values and philosophy of life. No wonder the early Christian writers described their struggles so frequently in terms of warfare. In the early Church Christians had to come together often to be strengthened and supported in their values and way of life since the world around them was pagan, its values so different, if not contrary, to their own.

Many contemporary authors refer to our era as "post-Christian," meaning after the era of Christian dominance and permeation. Basic values, once relatively unchallenged and generally accepted in the western hemisphere, are under fire. Massive efforts have been launched to destroy the family, heterosexuality, fidelity, marriage, permanent commitments, chastity, the rights of the unborn, handicapped, and the dying. Challenges to church life and community are felt daily.

Common today is the philosophy of life that sees humankind as born perfect, in need merely of being set free of the influences that have corrupted it, such as unwholesome environments, religious customs and rules, and the taboos generated by nonrational people.

Christians believe that humankind is basically good, but also tainted by evil and prone to rebellion. We need the redemptive power of Jesus to touch our lives, give us light and leadership, and bring us safely home to our Creator. This happens in the Christian family and in the community of believers, the Church.

1. One of the greatest gifts and responsibilities given by God to human beings is the power to choose, freedom.

Human beings could not love were it not for their freedom. One must be able to hate if one is to love; one must be able to choose the opposite of what is good if one is to be free to choose the good. The Reverence for Life and Family program concludes with a treatment of conscience and the choice that Christians have to make between various values. The theme throughout the course has been responsibility for one's choices. Another theme has been reverence, that is, the ability to treat someone or something according to its truth, as it ought to be treated. It should be obvious by now that, for the Christian, to appreciate the truth of God's creation and redeemed world is to establish the foundation for genuine responsibility. If responsibility means accountability, then the Christian is accountable ultimately to God.

In the Book of Genesis all created goods are called "good." What is truly human is the creation of God, and it is good. Jesus affirmed the goodness of life and of family; he affirmed the creation of His Father.

Genuine human values are also Christian values. A Christian value is one held by Jesus and His people. For example, marriage as a sacramental union is a specifically Christian value, marriage itself being a human value redeemed and raised to the level of sacrament by Jesus.

A "being" value is a creation of God, something of worth given by God and neither merited nor earned by us. It is not lost by any sin. A being value has an inherent value within itself and its worth can only be unveiled. It is not increased, nor can it be created or made by us. A being value is given by God. The Life and Family course has treated four being values. They are: (1) the dignity of the human person; (2) the maleness/femaleness of human persons, that is, sexuality; (3) the family; and (4) the Church. We will take a final look at each of these.

2. The human person has an intrinsic dignity.

Created "in the image of God" humans are capable of knowing and loving their Creator. The Creator appointed them to be master of all earthly creatures, subduing them and using them to God's glory. The person is composed of body and soul. The Church teaches in the Constitution on the Church in the Modern World:

> Through their bodily composition they gather to themselves the elements of the material world; thus they reach their crown through Him, and through Him raise their voice in free praise of the Creator. For this reason people are not allowed to despise their bodily life; rather they are obliged to regard their bodies as good and honorable since God has created them and will raise them up on the last day (no. 14).

God created the human soul to be spiritual and immortal. By the use of intellect the human person surpasses the material universe, sharing in the light of the divine mind. Not only does the person know, but the human person can choose. Another great power given to humankind is free will. In freedom the human person directs himself or herself toward goodness. It is essential to human dignity that freedom be real and actual.

The document goes on to say:

> For its part, authentic freedom is an exceptional sign of the divine image within humans. For God has willed that humans remain 'under control of their own decisions,' so that they can seek their creator spontaneously, and come freely to utter and blissful perfection through loyalty to Him. Hence human dignity demands that they act according to a knowing and free choice that is personally motivated and prompted from within, not under blind internal impulse nor by mere external pressure (no. 17).

The human person is called to emancipate him- or herself from all captivity to passion and to pursue God as goal, chosen as the good. Damaged by sin, the human person can reach God only by the aid of God's grace. Thus, human dignity does not reside only in the nature possessed by humans and created by

God, but it also resides in the redeemed quality of this same nature. Through redemption the human person becomes a child of God. And so the dignity of the human person is indeed great.

3. Not only did God create them in his own image, but he made them "male and female" (cf. Genesis 1:27). God did not create man to be alone.

By nature the human person is a social being and cannot survive nor develop as a human being apart from relationships to others. The human person is profoundly affected by sexuality. Sexuality, too, is a "being" value. It is not earned nor merited, nor is it lost by failure to use it well. Sexuality is a gift from God. It is not the creation of any creature. The person is either male or female, and together the two sexes comprise a marvelous complementarity, neither complete without the other.

4. A third "being" value is family.

Family is the creation of God and is the foundation of society. Again, a quotation from the Constitution on the Church in the Modern World is appropriate:

> Thus the family, in which the various generations come together and help one another grow wiser and harmonize personal rights with the other requirements of social life, is the foundation of society. All those, therefore, who exercise influence over communities and social groups should work effectively for the welfare of marriage and the family. Public authority should regard it as a sacred duty to recognize, protect and promote their authentic nature, to shield public morality, and to favor the prosperity of home life. The right of parents to beget and educate their children in the bosom of the family must be safeguarded. Children too who unhappily lack the blessing of a family should be protected by prudent legislation and various undertakings and assisted by the help they need (no. 52).

5. A fourth "being" value is Church. This creation of God is also a gift.

From the beginning of creation, God planned to raise human beings to a participation in the divine life. God did not leave us, fallen in Adam, but chose to redeem us in Jesus Christ. "He planned to assemble in the Holy Church all those who could believe in Christ" (Church in the Modern World, no. 2). In a real way the Church is the family of God.

6. These values in being find an immediate response in certain moral values.

The dignity of the person demands the moral value of *temperance*. That recognition of worth requires self-respect which in turn requires self-mastery. To sexuality corresponds the moral value of *chastity*. The qualities of maleness and femaleness and the fundamental vocation of marriage—even the other fundamental vocations of single life and single-vowed or celibate—require self-mastery in the area of sex. This is chastity. Family requires *married love* as its foundation. For the foundation of family is the promise made by each spouse to the other that he and she will be faithful, open to life, in a lasting relationship. Church demands our response of *faithfulness*. As God was faithful and is faithful and ever will be faithful, so divine faithfulness is the model for human faithfulness. Within the covenanted Church community all are called to be faithful to the Lord and thus to each other. Such faithfulness is empowering. Such faithfulness is the backbone for support in living out the Christian life.

Being Values	Moral Values
1. Person	Temperance
2. Sexuality	Chastity
3. Family	Married Love
4. Church	Faithfulness

A moral value is something of intrinsic moral goodness. The four moral values that we have been considering in the Reverence for Life and Family program are: (1) temperance; (2) chastity; (3) married love; and (4) faithfulness.

Temperance is that moral quality by which a person controls and moderates the desire for pleasurable things. It is self-mastery, self-discipline, and self-control. Temperance is practical. It regulates the use of food and drink, tobacco, drugs, and sex.

7. Chastity is the form of temperance which concerns itself with sexuality.

It is the form of self-discipline which controls the use of sex according to the divine plan. Chastity is a way of reverencing the male and female character of human beings. It restrains the movement of love according to what is good for the other person. In the letter to the Ephesians, chapter 5, St. Paul wrote:

> As for lewd conduct or promiscuousness or lust of any sort, let them not even be mentioned among you: your holiness forbids this. Nor should there by any obscene, or suggestive talk, all that is out of place. Instead give thanks. Make no mistake about this: no fornicator, no unclean or lustful person—in effect no idolater has any inheritance in the kingdom of Christ and of God.

All are called to chastity, whether married or single or vowed. Each Christian is called to use the power of sex rightly.

8. The third moral virtue we have been concerned about is the virtue of married love and fidelity.

God is the author of married love. He calls man and woman to a conjugal union whereby "two become one flesh." They are joined together in an irrevocable personal consent. As a man and a woman exchange their vows, God commits Himself to strengthen and to preserve that vow. The bond of marriage is obviously necessary for the rearing of children, providing the security that children need for their proper upbringing. Married love is total, human, faithful, and fruitful.

9. The Church is the People of God, a community born in the love of the Spirit, a people called to live life as Jesus did.

"Love one another as I have loved you" (John 15:12). With God as our Father, we stand in relation to one another as brothers and sisters in the Lord. We are called to be faithful, that is, to freely respond, with constancy, to the Lord who is our first love and to our neighbors as well. We cannot separate love of neighbor from love of God. Jesus teaches that there is but one commandment—love. Faithfulness remembers, does not forget, keeps in mind what the Lord has done. Faithfulness helps a person be constant in an attitude of thankfulness, of Eucharist.

Jesus came from the Father to redeem the world. While created as good, the world with humankind within it became "out of order" and needs to be restored, made over, redeemed. Everything is in need of redemption. The work of the Spirit is to make holy and to give new life, to restore all things in Christ. While moral values are there to be realized, they are not well perceived and cannot be lived, except by God's grace. All things, sexuality included, have been restored to their true place in the Father's plan through the saving action of Jesus and the sanctifying power of the Holy Spirit.

LESSON 15   LIST OF TERMS

Chastity
Form of temperance which regulates sexual desire and activity according to God's design.

Covenant Love
Formal, solemn, and binding; a relationship initiated by God and calling for a faith response from the people, freely given, faithful, and permanent.

Faith-Community
Body of believers, joined together by shared beliefs and values.

Integrated Sexuality
Sexuality expressed in harmony with all the powers of the whole person.

Marital Fidelity
Relationship between husband and wife is special and exclusive. Spouses promise to be faithful to each other, that is, to have a sexually intimate relationship with no one other than spouse.

Mutual Parenting
Shared in common. Mother and father share parenting responsibilities and roles.

Openness to Life
Husband and wife will accept children lovingly as gifts from God and give them a loving home in which to grow.

Permanent Commitment
Promise intended to be kept until death.

Person
Individual human being, created in the image of God.

Reverence
An attitude by which one treats someone or something as it should be treated, according to its beauty and truth; respecting creation according to the way God made it.

Sexuality
A gift from God which includes the complementary identities of male and female, and the potential capacity to relate and procreate according to one's identity.

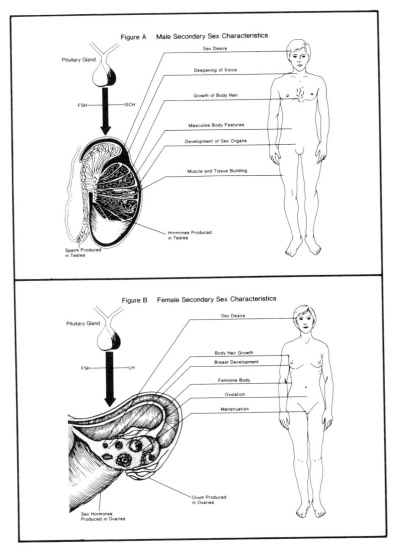

Figure A   Male Secondary Sex Characteristics

Pituitary Gland

FSH — ISCH

Sex Desire

Deepening of Voice

Growth of Body Hair

Masculine Body Features

Development of Sex Organs

Muscle and Tissue Building

Hormones Produced
in Testes

Sperm Produced
in Testes

Figure B   Female Secondary Sex Characteristics

Pituitary Gland

FSH — LH

Sex Desire

Body Hair Growth

Breast Development

Feminine Body

Ovulation

Menstruation

Ovum Produced
in Ovaries

Sex Hormones
Produced in Ovaries

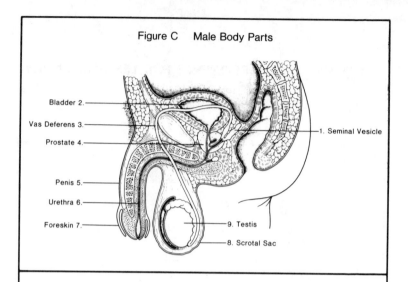

Figure C   Male Body Parts

Bladder 2.
Vas Deferens 3.
Prostate 4.
1. Seminal Vesicle
Penis 5.
Urethra 6.
Foreskin 7.
9. Testis
8. Scrotal Sac

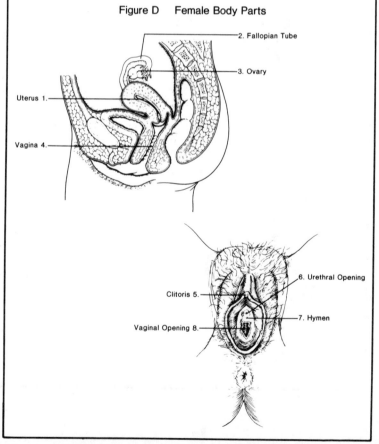

Figure D   Female Body Parts

2. Fallopian Tube
3. Ovary
Uterus 1.
Vagina 4.

6. Urethral Opening
Clitoris 5.
7. Hymen
Vaginal Opening 8.

MAJOR THEMES AND TOPICS
REVERENCE FOR LIFE AND FAMILY

The Reverence for Life and Family Program is comprised of two courses, one for parents and the other for ninth grade students. Thus, parents who view the materials first, are assisted in their responsibility as the prime educators of their children.

UNIT I	CHRISTIAN MARRIAGE AND FAMILY
Parent Session	Learning to reverence love, life, and family.
Student Sessions	1. "Christian Love and Marriage" Covenant love. Christian marriage. 2. "Born into Family and Church" Fetal development. Birth. Parenting. 3. "From Child to Adult" Adolescent growth. Reproductive systems.
UNIT II	INTEGRATION OF SEXUALITY
Parent Session	Learning to grow as a balanced, integrated person.
Student Sessions	4. "Sexual Integration and Wholeness" Integration. Spiritual growth. 5. "Self-Esteem and Intimacy" Self-esteem. Heterosexuality. Homosexuality. 6. "Challenge to Integration" Fears. Fantasies. Pornography. Masturbation.
UNIT III	RELATIONSHIPS AND RESPONSIBILITY
Parent Session	Learning to accept responsibilities connected with different kinds of relationships.
Student Sessions	7. "Responsibility for Relationships" Exploitation vs. covenant love. Unconditional love.

8. "Growing in Personal Relationships"
   Developing relationships. Dating.
9. "Serious Consequences of Sexual Activity"
   Venereal Disease. Teenage parenting.

UNIT IV   CHRISTIAN MORALITY
Parent Session   Learning to act according to principles of Christian morality.

Student Sessions   10. "The Choice for Chastity"
                               Morality. Chastity. Virginity.
                           11. "Essentials of Christian Marriage"
                               Responsible parenting. Conjugal love.
                           12. "Respect for Human Life"
                               Abortion. Respect life.

UNIT V   CHOOSING LIFE AND FAMILY VALUES
Parent Session   Learning to make moral choices.
Student Sessions   13. "Developing a Christian Conscience"
                               Conscience. Decision-making.
                           14. "Facing Peer Pressure"
                               Peer pressure. Societal influences.
                           15. "Life and Family Values"
                               Choosing Christian values.

UNIT I   **CHRISTIAN MARRIAGE AND FAMILY**
LESSON 1   **"CHRISTIAN LOVE AND MARRIAGE"**

VIDEO PROGRAM   Unit I, Part 1: "Christian Marriage and Covenant Love"

CONCEPT   God has first loved us and calls us to loving relationship and community.

ATTITUDES   *The student will be exposed to the following values and feelings:*
                           *Life is a gift, is precious and deserving of reverence.
                           *Good family life is essential to a stable society.
                           *Conjugal love, i.e., the love of husband and wife, is blessed by God.

150

God invites human persons to share in the creation of new life.

Every person has dignity and worth.

SKILLS

The student will be able to:

*Explain that God is the author of the marriage bond.

*Show how Christian marriage is modeled after God's covenant with the chosen people (a bond of love and fidelity).

*Define "reverence" and give examples of both the presence and absence of it in daily life.

*List fidelity, permanence, and openness to life (children) as essential aspects of marriage, and explain them.

Define or describe terms: *family, marriage, covenant, reverence, relationship, conjugal love, fidelity, community, openness to life* (children), *permanence.*

Know rules for communication and class conduct.

KNOWLEDGE

The student will consider these concepts and principles:

God is love—Father, Son and Spirit in a relationship of love.

*God has first loved us, a revelation given especially in the covenant with Israel and in Jesus' love for the Church.

The human person is made in God's image, empowered to love.

*God is the author of the marriage bond.

*Parents are cooperators with the love of God the Creator.

Children are the supreme gift of marriage.

*The family is a community of love.

*Christian marriage symbolizes God's love for the chosen people, a faithful and permanent love.

*Reverence is the ability to treat someone or something as it should be treated, according to its own beauty and truth.

*Major emphasis

151

UNIT I **LESSON 2**	**CHRISTIAN MARRIAGE AND FAMILY** **"BORN INTO FAMILY AND** **CHURCH"**
VIDEO PROGRAM	Unit I, Part 2: "First Days of Life," Part 3: "Birth of Water and the Spirit"
CONCEPT	The Christian community, through Baptism, receives and welcomes the newborn child, who was created through a remarkable process of God's design and with both parents becoming co-creators with God.
ATTITUDES	*The student will be exposed to the following values and feelings:* *Giving birth is a privilege and a responsibility. *Parenting is a mutual responsibility for mother and father. *Children are especially impressionable. *Children have the best opportunities for development in the environment of a stable home and marriage (cradle of love). Pregnancy brings responsibility for another life to the expectant parents. *Responsibilities of parenthood require preparation and maturity. *Every child has a right to have a mother and father.
SKILLS	*The student will be able to:* *Describe the desired qualities for a "community of love," whether in the home or in the Church. *Show that "procreation" is more than reproduction. *Describe what is meant by mutual parenting. Define the terms: *birth canal, conception, fertilization, legal age, mutual parenting, ovum, pregnancy, procreation, reproduction, semen, sperm, vagina.*

152

KNOWLEDGE

The student will consider these concepts and principles:

*Baptism is birth into the people of God.

*God has designed a remarkable process for development of life in the womb.

*Some children are placed in the care of adoptive parents who love them as their own.

Conception is the point at which new life begins.

Experiences of the pregnant mother directly influence the developing baby.

The father of the child can participate actively in the birthing process.

The first years of life are times of lifelong influences.

*The father of the child is as responsible as the mother for the child's care.

A child is legally under the care and supervision of the parents until majority age.

*A Christian child belongs to two communities of love, family and Church.

*Major emphasis

UNIT I
LESSON 3

CHRISTIAN MARRIAGE AND FAMILY
"FROM CHILD TO ADULT"

VIDEO PROGRAM

Unit I, Part 4: "Secondary Sex Characteristics," Part 5: "Male and Female Reproductive Systems"

CONCEPT

During adolescence a person experiences remarkable physical and emotional growth, and it is a time given by God to especially appreciate one's sexuality and the moral qualities required to reverence it.

ATTITUDES

The student will be exposed to the following values and feelings:

*Using correct terminology is appropriate in discussing sex and sexuality.

*Adolescence is a normal and necessary stage of growth designed by God.

*Physical changes and emotional changes are interrelated.

God's creation is a wonder.

SKILLS

The student will be able to:

*List the major physical and psychosocial changes which occur in adolescence.

*Describe the male and female reproductive system using the proper terminology.

Define or describe terms: *ejaculation, erection, genitalia, hormone, implantation, labor, menopause, menstruation, miscarriage, ovulation, pituitary gland, placenta, puberty, sexual intercourse, umbilical cord, wet dreams.*

KNOWLEDGE

The student will consider these concepts and principles:

*Adolescence is a time of great physical and psychosocial change.

*The male and female reproductive system is one of the major human body systems.

Different rates of growth between individuals are normal during adolescence.

Responsibility accompanies the opportunity to participate in adult behavior.

*Primary sex characteristics identify a person as male or female and are present at birth; they are reproductive organs.

*Secondary sex characteristics are those that appear at puberty, e.g., sex desire, growth of body hair, development of sex organs.

*Menstruation (girls) and wet dreams (boys) are normal occurrences in adolescence once puberty begins.

Physical sexual maturity occurs for the most part without choice, while emotional, social, and moral maturity depend to some degree on individual choice.

*Major emphasis

UNIT II	INTEGRATION OF SEXUALITY
LESSON 4	"SEXUAL INTEGRATION AND
	WHOLENESS"

VIDEO PROGRAM   Unit II, Part 1: "Called to Wholeness," Part 2: "Spiritual Growth in Adolescence"

CONCEPT   God calls every person to try to achieve wholeness. Personal wholeness and holiness are augmented by actively trying to develop a balanced life, by growing in moderation, and by seeking ways to be open to self, friends, family, and God.

ATTITUDES   *The student will be exposed to the following values and feelings:*
*Moderation is an expression of reverence for life.
*God calls every person to try to achieve wholeness.
Self-control is a positive contributor toward wholesome growth.
*The most significant insight a person can experience is that he or she is truly and personally loved by God.
Each person has a place in the Christian community.

SKILLS   *The student will be able to:*
*Describe how integration is the goal of a fulfilled life.
*Contrast the actions and behaviors that lead to or away from the wholeness and integration to which God calls each person.
*Recognize that among the most significant insights a person can experience is that she or he is truly and personally loved by God, invited to a personal relationship with God and called to the community of the Church.
Define terms: *balance, genitality, integration, moderation, over-indulgence, preoccupation, self-development, self-restraint, sexuality, sin, virtue, wholeness.*

KNOWLEDGE

The student will consider these concepts and principles:

*Integration is the process of making whole, bringing about a unity.

*Sexuality is that dimension of the person which makes a person male or female, capable of affective bonds and procreative activity.

Genitality is the biological, physical, reproductive dimension of sexuality, which includes arousal and orgasm.

Sin is the deliberate turning away from God.

Integration is especially a life task for youth and young adults, but remains a task through adulthood.

*We need to grow in our relationship with God. Jesus taught the importance of the individual. We learn to be with and communicate with God in new adult ways.

*Moderation is the avoidance of extremes and excesses of any kind.

*Major emphasis

UNIT II
LESSON 5

INTEGRATION OF SEXUALITY
"SELF-ESTEEM AND INTIMACY"

VIDEO PROGRAM

Unit II, Part 3: "Self-Worth and Acceptance," Part 4: "The Church's Teaching on Homosexuality"

CONCEPT

Although every person is a unique creation of God, no person is perfect. Christians believe that every person is basically good and worthwhile but yearns for the complete fulfillment made possible by Jesus' redemptive act.

ATTITUDES

The student will be exposed to the following values and feelings:

*Every person is worthwhile in God's eyes.

*Some things can't be changed and must be accepted.

*Looking at weaknesses is easy, but it is important to look at strengths.

What is most important is that which is invisible to the eye.
Homosexuals are persons with human needs and rights.
Christians avoid passing judgment on anyone's relationship to God.

SKILLS

The student will be able to:
List personal good points and strengths.
Explain difference between changeable and unchangeable aspects of personality and make-up.
Distinguish homosexual orientation from homosexual activity.
Define or describe terms: *esteem, gay, heterosexuality, homosexual activity, homosexuality, homosexual orientation, human dignity, human rights, intimacy, lesbian, self-acceptance, self-image, self-respect, self-worth.*

KNOWLEDGE

The student will consider these concepts and principles:
*Every person is a unique creation of God.
Physical appearance can be enhanced.
*Relationships with persons of the same and/or the opposite sex can enhance or delay self-worth and integration.
Vast majority of persons are heterosexual; a minority are homosexual.
Not everything is known or understood about homosexuality.
*Homosexual orientation is not immoral; homosexual activity is immoral.
*Like all persons, homosexuals need human relationships and deserve the care and warmth of the Church.
*Homosexuals have the same human rights as anyone else.
A person greatly bothered by sexuality questions or problems is well-advised to seek counsel.

*Major emphasis

INTEGRATION OF SEXUALITY "CHALLENGES TO INTEGRATION"

VIDEO PROGRAM

Unit II, Part 5: "Some Challenges to Adolescent Growth"

CONCEPT

Genuine love is other-centered. Persons striving to become sexually integrated want to avoid sexual expression and activity that are self-centered.

ATTITUDES

The student will be exposed to the following values and feelings:
*Each person can meet challenges and grow from them.
*No sin is beyond the forgiving power of God.
*Perfect integration is a lifelong goal.
Sex is precious and good and not something to be cheapened.
Some sexual thoughts and actions are disintegrating and to be avoided.

SKILLS

The student will be able to:
*Distinguish between helpful and harmful fantasies and fears.
*Recognize negative effects of pornography on wholesome development.
*Summarize the Church's teaching on masturbation.
Define or describe: *compulsion, impotence, integration, lust, masturbation, obscenity, pornography, preoccupation, sexual fantasy, sexual fear, sterility, temperance.*

KNOWLEDGE

The student will consider these concepts and principles:
*Sexual fantasies and sexual fears can be helpful or harmful to growth.
*The Church teaches that masturbation is morally wrong since it violates the two essential purposes of sexual power, namely, procreation and the marriage relationship.

*At times, counsel should be sought so a person may achieve greater integration.

Sex usually begins in the brain (imagination and desire).

Many well-intentioned people today contribute to the cheapening of sex, especially through pornography.

*Major emphasis

UNIT III	**RELATIONSHIPS AND RESPONSIBILITIES**
LESSON 7	**"RESPONSIBILITY FOR RELATIONSHIPS"**

VIDEO PROGRAM
: Unit III, Part 1, "Examining Relationships"

CONCEPT
: Personal relationships vary in kind and quality. Reflection on relationships helps a person assess and evaluate the capacity of genuine love.

ATTITUDES
: *The student will be exposed to the following values and feelings:*
Exploitation is to be avoided.
Infatuation is not reason enough for marriage.
Keeping one's promises in little things makes it possible to do so in bigger things.
*Keeping one's word is important.
*Betrayal of trust can cause serious hurt.
True friendship is founded upon something of value and promotes mutual welfare.

SKILLS
: *The student will be able to:*
*Distinguish between *exploitation, friendship, infatuation* and *committed love*.
*Analyze relationships, pointing out both positive and negative aspects.
Define or describe terms: *affection, commitment, covenant love, exploitation, friendship, infatuation, personal relationship, responsibility, sacrificial love,* and *unconditional love*.

159

The student will consider these concepts and principles:

*Some characteristics of friendship are: mutual giving, trust, reliability, loyalty, respect, compassion, truthfulness.

Some characteristics of infatuation are: fantasy, unreality, dream world.

Some characteristics of exploitation are: selfishness, taking without giving, using others as objects.

*Some characteristics of committed love are: permanence, giving without taking, caring, understanding.

*Friendship and committed love are goods to be sought.

God's love for us is unconditional.

*Major emphasis

UNIT III

LESSON 8

RELATIONSHIPS AND RESPONSIBILITIES

"GROWING IN PERSONAL RELATIONSHIPS"

VIDEO PROGRAM

Unit III, Part 2: "Learning to Date"

CONCEPT

Adolescents move from group experiences to dating experiences. They need to explore the purposes and benefits of dating and should set standards for themselves.

ATTITUDES

The student will be exposed to the following values and feelings:

*Sex is for life.

Dating can be a significant experience and should be taken seriously.

*Not all teenagers are ready for dating experiences at the same age.

Choosing not to date or go steady is okay.

*Dating for the young person is a remote but necessary preparation for marriage.

SKILLS	*The student will be able to:*

The student will be able to:
*Identify and describe the benefits of dating.
*List a personal set of standards for dating.
*Describe the principal purposes of dating.
Define or describe terms: *dating, exclusiveness, "going with," group experiences, honesty, independence, interactions, socialization, standards, value.*

KNOWLEDGE

The student will consider these concepts and principles: .
*The Catholic Church has traditionally taught that sexual activity between persons of the two sexes is to be personal, honest, responsible, and open to life.
Dating fulfills some needs of adolescents: independence, identity, enjoyment, relationship.
*Dating enhances a person by enhancing self-image and improving relationship with God.
*Relationships should be governed by certain standards or rules.
A major purpose of dating is learning to relate to persons of the opposite sex.
Since wholesome relationships are essential to human fulfillment, learning to relate is necessary for those who remain single as well as those who marry.

*Major emphasis

UNIT III

RELATIONSHIPS AND RESPONSIBILITIES

LESSON 9

"SERIOUS CONSEQUENCES OF SEXUAL ACTIVITY"

VIDEO PROGRAM

Unit III, Part 3: "Venereal Disease"; Part 4: "Teenage Pregnancy"

CONCEPT

People are responsible for their actions. One of the ways teenagers can develop personal responsibility is by realizing the serious consequences of sexual activity.

161

ATTITUDES	*The student will be exposed to the following values and feelings:*
	*Growing into adulthood gradually and well is better than growing too fast and poorly.
	Some common peer attitudes toward sex are harmful.
	Though sex can be enjoyable, it is not "for fun," a plaything.
	*People are responsible for their actions.
SKILLS	*The student will be able to:*
	*Identify and critique from a Christian perspective four common contemporary attitudes toward sex.
	*List the major medical effects of venereal disease.
	*Describe the problems and difficulties associated with teenage parenting.
	Define or describe terms: *genital herpes, gonorrhea, herpes simplex, herpes II, moral norm, parenting, pregnancy testing, prenatal care, single parent, sterilization, syphilis, teenage parenting, venereal disease.*
KNOWLEDGE	*The student will consider these concepts and principles:*
	*Feelings and emotions are not adequate in themselves to serve as moral guides.
	*Some human activity can have long range negative effects, though the immediate effects may appear to be harmless.
	Although sex can be pleasurable and enjoyable, it is not to be treated lightly or merely as a plaything.
	*Two serious problems caused by sexual activity are venereal disease and teenage parenting.
	*For the sexually active adolescent, VD can result in blindness, brain damage, heart defects, disfigurement, and possibly death.
	Teenagers are not yet ready to be parents.
	Teenagers who need help or guidance can turn to the Church for assistance.
	*Major emphasis

162

UNIT IV LESSON 10	**CHRISTIAN MORALITY** **"THE CHOICE FOR CHASTITY"**
VIDEO PROGRAM	Unit IV, Part 1: "Morality of Premarital Sex and Intercourse"
CONCEPT	Chastity is essential for growth in genuine love. Teenagers are capable of self-restraint, self-mastery, and self-control.
ATTITUDES	*The student will be exposed to the following values and feelings:* *Christians are challenged to "dare to be different" in today's culture. Not to be sexually active is okay. *Resisting peer pressure which pushes teenagers toward sexual intimacy is good. Virginity and chastity are for men as well as women. *A contraceptive mentality sells teenagers short, as if they are the first generation that can't be self-disciplined and self-controlled.
SKILLS	*The student will be able to:* *State and explain the norms the Church gives for sexual moral behavior. *List five or six reasons why a person should "wait until marriage." *Tell the Gospel story of the woman caught in adultery. Define or describe terms: *adultery, contraceptive mentality, chastity, fornication, premarital intercourse, premarital sex, "premature bonding," virginity.*
KNOWLEDGE	*The student will consider these concepts and principles:* *Sexual intercourse is morally right only in marriage. *Sexual activity preparing for intercourse belongs in marriage.

*Fidelity is the giving oneself totally and exclusively to one's spouse.

*Permanency is the giving oneself to one's spouse until death.

*Openness to life is the capacity to accept children lovingly from God.

*Virginity at the time of marriage says sex is something special to be shared only with spouse.

*Teenagers are capable of self-restraint, self-mastery and self-control.

Fornication is sexual intercourse outside of marriage between the unmarried.

Adultery is sexual intercourse by a married person with a person other than a spouse.

*Major emphasis

UNIT IV **LESSON 11**	**CHRISTIAN MORALITY** **"ESSENTIALS OF CHRISTIAN MARRIAGE"**
VIDEO PROGRAM	Unit IV, Part 2: "An Intimate Partnership"
CONCEPT	Marriage is an intimate partnership of life and love. Husband and wife together are responsible for the achievement of the unitive and procreative purposes of marriage.
ATTITUDES	*The student will be exposed to the following values and feelings:*

*Christian marriage takes effort on the part of both husband and wife.

Marriage is a union of minds and hearts and bodies.

*Children are gifts from God.

"Unplanned pregnancies" can become "wanted children."

*The greatest gift a father can give a child is to love the child's mother. The same is true for the mother.

*Having a family requires much communication, preparation, and prayer.

The student will be able to:
*List and describe the two coessential purposes of marriage.
*List the factors to be considered in planning to have a family.
*List the criteria to be considered in choosing a method of family planning.
*List some of the ways youth can prepare themselves to be capable of responsibility to the unitive and procreative demands of marriage.
Define or describe terms: *abstinence, conception, contraceptives, fertility, mutuality, natural family planning, procreative purpose, responsible parenthood, unitive purpose.*

KNOWLEDGE   *The student will treat these concepts and principles:*
*Marriage has two essential purposes, the bringing of children into the world (procreative) and the mutual love of the spouses (unitive).
Children are the supreme gift of marriage.
*Responsible parenting includes preparing and deciding to have a child, conceiving and bearing the child, and rearing and educating the child.
*Responsible marriage relationship includes the primacy of the spouse, communication, mutual respect and mutual nurturing.
*The ovulation method and the sympto-thermic method are natural means of family planning which are consistent with the Church's teaching.

*Major emphasis

UNIT IV
LESSON 12

CHRISTIAN MORALITY
"RESPECT FOR HUMAN LIFE"

VIDEO PROGRAM   Unit IV, Part 3: "Abortion and Life Issues"

CONCEPT   Life is a gift and a responsibility and is precious from conception until death.

ATTITUDES	*The students will be exposed to the following values and feelings:*
	*No one can set a price tag on a human person. Every person has a right to life from conception to death.
	Adoption lists are long, showing that no child is unwanted, only misplaced.
	*Because something is legal it doesn't make it moral.
	*Respect for life means respect for life at every age and condition.
SKILLS	*The student will be able to:*
	*Define abortion and explain the Church's teaching on the morality of abortion.
	*Describe the broader confines of "respect for life," that is, respect at every age and condition.
	*Describe how abortion is legal in the U.S. but immoral from the Church's point of view.
	Define or describe: *abortion, Caesarian section, euthanasia, fetus, incest, infanticide, Judaeo-Christian ethic, murder, neonate, rape, suicide.*
KNOWLEDGE	*The student will treat these concepts and principles:*
	*Life is a gift and a responsibility.
	*Each person is valuable regardless of age or condition.
	*Life is precious at every stage, from conception to death.
	Abortion has some physical and emotional side effects which can be serious.
	A mother's right to privacy is subordinate to a child's right to life.
	Birthright and local health care centers provide alternatives to abortion.
	*Although abortion is legal as of 1973 in the U.S., the Catholic Church teaches that abortion is gravely immoral.
	*Major emphasis

UNIT V

LESSON 13

CHOOSING LIFE AND
FAMILY VALUES
"DEVELOPING A CHRISTIAN
CONSCIENCE"

VIDEO PROGRAM   Unit V, Part 1: "A Model for Decision Making"

CONCEPT   Conscience requires development. The basic
                  sense of morality "is written on our hearts," but
                  needs to be correctly informed, wisely advised,
                  and spiritually motivated.

ATTITUDES   *The student will be exposed to the following
                  values and feelings:*
                  *People are responsible for their decisions and
                  actions.
                  *Consciences are formed and developed.
                  People can learn and grow from their mistakes
                  and even from their sins.
                  *God is the ultimate goal of all human activity.
                  The Christian is called to respond to God's love
                  at all times.

SKILLS   *The student will be able to:*
                  *Outline and explain the steps involved in mak-
                  ing an informed moral decision.
                  *Define *conscience* and describe what is meant
                  by the term "Christian conscience."
                  *Explain the role that values play in making
                  moral decisions.
                  *Show how values are expressed in laws.
                  Define or describe the terms: *conscience, Chris-
                  tian conscience, guidance, guilt, ideal law,
                  moral act, moral judgment, moral norm, re-
                  sponsibility, sin, value.*

KNOWLEDGE   *The student will consider these concepts and
                  principles:*
                  *Christian conscience is in tune with the values
                  and principles of Jesus.

*Ideals are the values a person holds as important in life.

*Value is someone or something prized or esteemed. It is that which is held dear and considered of worth.

Moral norm is a standard or criterion expressing morally right behavior. It expresses the good as intended by the Creator (natural moral law).

A right, moral act is any human activity which is done in accord with the moral law and in good conscience.

Sin is the deliberate refusal to live according to God's plan as one knows it. Sin is going against one's conscience.

Guidance is the assistance given or sought which helps a person discover the moral good.

Laws are precise formulations of moral norms.

*Conscience is the intellect making a judgment about the rightness or wrongness of a particular action.

*Major emphasis

UNIT V	**CHOOSING LIFE AND FAMILY VALUES**
LESSON 14	**"FACING PEER PRESSURE"**

VIDEO PROGRAM	Unit V, Part 3, "Reflections on Peer Pressure"
CONCEPT	Three of the greatest gifts from God are human life, human family, and the faith—family we call Church.
ATTITUDES	*The student will be exposed to the following values and feelings:*

Every person is responsible for the quality of life.

*Giving in to peer pressure can be constructive or destructive.

*Prayer and a faith relationship with God are powerful helps for living out Christian values.

*Young people need children and adults; adults need young people and children.

Family values will be lost if people do not cherish them.

SKILLS

The student will be able to:

Explain the term "peer pressure" and describe how music, teenage fads and fashions, institutional structures and various antiauthority movements affect youths' personal dignity and freedom.

Identify three positive and three negative peer pressures relating to Christian moral positions.

Explain how the Church teaches life and family values and provides support for them.

Define or describe terms: *Christian values, Church, counsel, family values, life values, peer, peer pressure, support for values, witnessing.*

KNOWLEDGE

The student will consider these concepts and principles:

*Christians find support from one another in living out Christian life and family values.

*Church members are responsible for one another.

*Youth may seek counsel and support from parents, teachers, and clergy.

*Participation in the sacramental life of the Church teaches and supports Christian values.

Peer pressures can be constructive or destructive.

Peer pressure reduces freedom and destroys individuality.

Every person is responsible for his or her own life.

Contemporary society often denies parents their rightful role in guiding their children.

*Major emphasis

UNIT V	CHOOSING LIFE AND
	FAMILY VALUES
LESSON 15	"LIFE AND FAMILY VALUES"

VIDEO PROGRAM — Unit V, Part 3, "Choosing Christian Values"

CONCEPT — The Christian person is called to choose life and family values. First one appreciates the value, then says "yes" to it, and finally acts accordingly.

ATTITUDES — *The student will be exposed to the following values and feelings:*

Life is a gift from God.

*Christian values are worth striving for and they greatly enrich human experience.

*Jesus is the way, the truth, and the life.

*Christians must face the choices between Christian values and opposing values.

SKILLS — *The student will be able to:*

*List and describe ten values that flow from God's gifts of life and family.

*Describe in own words the meaning of *reverence*, giving examples of ways in which life and family values are reverenced.

KNOWLEDGE — *The student will consider these concepts and principles:*

*A Christian way of life is life lived according to the teachings and values of Jesus Christ.

*Christian marriage and family are two of God's special creations and gifts.

*Learning to relate to other people in wholesome ways is one of the tasks God gives to adolescents.

Sexuality is a precious gift from God.

*The choices we make determine the quality of our life experience.

*Major emphasis